GOOD INTENTIONS

NOTE

This book contains the whole of the verses published in the United States of America under the title *Good Intentions*, together with a number of poems from the author's earlier volumes.

GOOD INTENTIONS

BY OGDEN NASH

LONDON: J. M. DENT & SONS LTD.

BOOK
PRODUCTION
WAR ECONOMY
STANDARD

CONTENTS

Contents

Contents

Contents

Contents

Contents

Contents

Allow Me, Madam, but It Won't Help

Adorable is an adjective and womankind is a noun,

And I often wonder why, although adorable womankind elects to talk standing up, it elects to put on its coat sitting down.

What is the outstanding characteristic of matinées, tea rooms and table d'hôtes?

Women, sitting firmly and uncomfortably on their coats;

Women at whose talents a contortionist would hesitate to scoff,

Because they also sat down on their coats to take them off.

What is *savoir faire*?

It is the ability to pick up eighty-five cents in nickels and a lipstick with the right hand while the left hand is groping wildly over the back of a chair.

Yes, and if you desire *savoir faire* that you could balance a cup on,

Consider the calmness of a woman trying to get
    her arm into the sleeve of a coat that she has
    sat down on too far up on.
Women are indeed the salt of the earth,
But I fail to see why they daily submit themselves
    voluntarily to an operation that a man only
    undergoes when he is trying to put on his
    trousers in an upper berth.

Two and One *Are* a Problem

Dear Miss Dix, I am a young man of half-past
    thirty-seven.
My friends say I am not unattractive, though to be
    kind and true is what I have always striven.
I have brown hair, green eyes, a sensitive mouth
    and a winning natural exuberance,
And, at the waist, a barely noticeable protuberance.
I am open-minded about beverages so long as they
    are grape, brandy or malt,
And I am generous to practically any fault.
Well Miss Dix not to beat around the bush, there is
    a certain someone who thinks I am pretty nice,

And I turn to you for advice.

You see, it started when I was away on the road

And returned to find a pair of lovebirds had taken up their abode in my abode.

Well I am not crazy about lovebirds, but I must say they looked very sweet in their gilded cage,

And their friendship had reached an advanced stage,

And I had just forgiven her who of the feathered fiancés was the donor of

When the houseboy caught a lost lovebird in the yard that we couldn't locate the owner of.

So then we had three, and it was no time for flippancy,

Because everybody knows that a lovebird without its own lovebird to love will pine away and die of the discrepancy,

So we bought a fourth lovebird for the third lovebird and they sat around very cozily beak to beak

And then the third lovebird that we had provided the fourth lovebird for to keep it from dying died at the end of the week,

So we were left with an odd lovebird and it was
    no time for flippancy,
Because a lovebird without its own lovebird to
    love will pine away and die of the discrepancy,
So we had to buy a fifth lovebird to console the
    fourth love bird that we had bought to keep
    the third lovebird contented,
And now the fourth lovebird has lost its appetite,
    and, Miss Dix, I am going demented.
I don't want to break any hearts, but I got to know
    where I'm at;
Must I keep on buying lovebirds, Miss Dix, or do
    you think it would be all right to buy a cat?

The City

Here men walk alone
For most of their lives,
What with hydrants for dogs,
And windows for wives.

What is life? Life is stepping down a step or
    sitting in a chair,
And it isn't there.
Life is not having been told that the man has just
    waxed the floor,
It is pulling doors marked Push and pushing doors
    marked Pull and not noticing notices which
    say Please Use Other Door.
Life is an Easter Parade
In which you whisper: ' No darling if it 's a boy
    we 'll name him after your father! ' into the
    ear of an astonished stranger because the lady
    you thought was walking beside you has
    stopped to gaze into a window full of
    radishes and hot malted lemonade.
It is when you diagnose a sore throat as an un-
    prepared geography lesson and send your
    child weeping to school only to be returned
    an hour later covered with spots that are in-
    dubitably genuine,
It is a concert with a trombone soloist filling in
    for Yehudi Menuhin.

Were it not for frustration and humiliation
I suppose the human race would get ideas above
  its station.
Somebody once described Shelley as a beautiful
  and ineffective angel beating his luminous
  wings against the void in vain,
Which is certainly describing with might and main,
But probably means that we are all brothers under
  our pelts,
And Shelley went around pulling doors marked
  Push and pushing doors marked Pull just like
  everybody else.

Glossina Morsitans, or, the Tsetse

A Glossina morsitans bit rich Aunt Betsy,
Tsk tsk, tsetse.

Now Tell Me About Yourself

Everybody speaks of being patronized,
Yet nobody speaks of the truly irksome shambles
  which is, or are, being matronized,

By which I mean that there is nothing more im-
politely and noticeably aloof
Than a woman of a certain sort sounding out a
man of whose certain sort she hasn't yet got
definite affidavits or proof.
She displays the great names of her acquaintance
for his benefit like a *nouveau riche* displaying his
riches,
And fixes him with the stare of a psychiatrist to
see if there is one at which he twitches.
George Washington and George Sand and Lloyd
George to her are Georgie,
And she would have addressed the Borgias behind
their backs as Borgie.
She always wants to know, first, where do you
come from, and second, do you of course
know Babs and Bonzo Beaver there, which
you never do, often for your own very good
reasons, but you try to make your reply a
polite one,
So you murmur: ' Well I don't really know them,
but I know of them,' and she at once assigns
you to your proper side of the tracks, and it
is not the right one.

When she discusses national affairs she doesn't talk
    exactly treasonably,
But she refers to that part of the nation which lies
    outside of New York in the bright tone of one
    referring to a little tailor she has just dis-
    covered who does alterations very reasonably.
Please do not get the impression that a matronizing
    woman causes me to froth at the mouth or slaver;
I only wish to notify you that whenever you want
    her you can have her.

Lather As You Go

Beneath this slab
John Brown is stowed.
He watched the ads,
And not the road.

The Strange Case of the Girl o' Mr. Sponsoon's Dreams

Once upon a time there was a man named Mr.
    Sponsoon who was highly ineffectual.

He always looked as if he were growing a mustache.

His singing voice was pretty fair except for the high notes.

Oh yes, and the low notes, too.

One day he was driving along the street when he saw a beautiful girl.

My, what a beautiful girl, said Mr. Sponsoon, I wish I knew her name.

If I asked her her name, said Mr. Sponsoon, she might think me a brazen cad.

But if I don't know her name, she will go out of my life for ever.

Mr. Sponsoon thought and thought.

Suppose I run over her gently, he thought at last.

With one wheel, say.

Certainly with no more than two.

Then I can read her name in the morning paper and all will be hotsy-totsy.

Mr. Sponsoon pointed his car at the beautiful girl.

The beautiful girl leaped like a thoroughbred gazelle.

Mr. Sponsoon chased her for seven blocks and never laid a wheel on her.

In the middle of the eighth block she stopped to moisten her finger on account of a run in her stocking.

Mr. Sponsoon read in the morning paper that her name was Shella Schminck and she was in Percy's Hospital.

So he went to the Mercy Hospital and asked for Stella Smith.

To the girl o' his dreams he explained his little stratagem.

Girl o' my dreams, I had to know your name, said Mr. Sponsoon, avoiding high notes and low notes.

Say you forgive me, girl o' my dreams.

Say all is hotsy-totsy.

The girl o' Mr. Sponsoon's dreams said all was far from hotsy-totsy.

All was coldsy-toldsy, said the girl of Mr. Sponsoon's dreams.

Mr. Sponsoon joined the Foreign Legion, but was soon expelled because he admitted he liked it.

When last heard of, he was borrowing a burnt cork from Amos and Andy.

He said he had decided to steal into Rome as an Ethiopian spy.

Tin Wedding Whistle

Though you know it anyhow
Listen to me, darling, now,

Proving what I need not prove
How I know I love you, love.

11

Near and far, near and far,
I am happy where you are;

Likewise I have never larnt
How to be it where you aren't.

Far and wide, far and wide,
I can walk with you beside;

Furthermore, I tell you what,
I sit and sulk where you are not.

Visitors remark my frown
When you 're upstairs and I am down,

Yes, and I 'm afraid I pout
When I 'm indoors and you are out;

But how contentedly I view
Any room containing you.

In fact I care not where you be,
Just as long as it 's with me.

In all your absences I glimpse
Fire and flood and trolls and imps.

Is your train a minute slothful?
I goad the stationmaster wrothful.

When with friends to bridge you drive
I never know if you're alive.

And when you linger late in shops
I long to telephone the cops.

Yet how worth the waiting for,
To see you coming through the door.

Somehow, I can be complacent
Never but with you adjacent.

Near and far, near and far,
I am happy where you are;

Likewise, I have never larnt
How to be it where you aren't.

Then grudge me not my fond endeavor,
To hold you in my sight for ever;

Let none, not even you, disparage
Such valid reason for a marriage.

The Skink

Let us do justice to the skink
Who isn't what so many think.
On consultation with a wizard
I find the skink a kind of lizard.
Since he is not a printer's whim,
Don't sniff and back away from him,
Or you may be adjudged too drunk
To tell a lizard from a skunk.

The Strange Case of Mr. Ormantude's Bride

Once there was a bridegroom named Mr. Orman-
    tude whose intentions were hard to disparage,
Because he intended to make his a happy marriage,
And he succeeded for going on fifty years,
During which he was in marital bliss up to his ears.
His wife's days and nights were enjoyable
Because he catered to every foible;
He went around humming hymns
And anticipating her whims.
Many a fine bit of repartee died on his lips
Lest it throw her anecdotes into eclipse;

He was always silent when his cause was meri-
    torious,
And he never engaged in argument unless sure
    he was so obviously wrong that she couldn't
    help emerging victorious,
And always when in her vicinity
He was careful to make allowances for her
    femininity;
Were she snappish, he was sweetish,
And of understanding her he made a fetish.
Everybody said his chances of celebrating his
    golden wedding looked good,
But on his golden wedding eve he was competently
    poisoned by his wife who could no longer
    stand being perpetually understood.

The *Absentees*

I'd ride a cock horse to Banbury Cross
For giblet gravy and cranberry sauce,
Two treats which are held in reserve by the waiter
Till you've finished your turkey and mashed
    potater.

Dear Mr. Collector: In years gone by
Few have loved you as little as I,
Or lifted their voices and torn their raiment
And so begrudged the quarterly payment.
We waged our feud with ferocious joy,
You the Hatfield, I the McCoy.
Before December Seventh, you see,
You were You and I was Me,
But since the little men willed it thus,
Why, suddenly You and I are Us,
Just as Internal Revenue
To-day is Internal Combustion, too.
Enclosed find check, my unseen friend,
And never was check more gladly penned.
It is somewhat less than an emperor's ransom,
But cash it quickly and spend it handsome;
Spend it on factory, fort or farm,
Wherever you feel it will do most harm,
For I 'd like to export a present to Nippon;
Buy me a present, and make it a pippin.
We sent some gifts in twenty-three,
When their cities were crushed between earth and sea,

But merely nurses and doctors and food
To bind their wounds and foster their brood.
Their letter of thanks was suave and pleasant
But this time, please, a more practical present,
A gift to be truly honoured by
The truly honourable Samurai.
Consider how, nineteen years ago,
The children wept in Tokyo.
The little children hungered and bled.
The children were healed and clothed and
fed.
The children had reason to understand
American heart, American hand.
Which of the children, I wonder, grew
To fly in the shadow of Kurusu?
An ingenious race are the Nipponese,
Their secret weapon, a flag of peace.
Mr. Collector, I ask again,
Buy me a gift for the little men,
Let me pay for part of a Boeing,
Keep a Martin or Douglas going,
Put the money wherever you choose,
In guns or rivets or hobnailed shoes—
Now I know what money is for,

It 's going to let me into the war.
Here 's my admission.   Need to hike it?
Hit me again, my friend, I like it!

The Louse

Robert Burns, that gifted souse,
Kindly immortalized the louse,
Who probably won't, when he is master,
Immortalize this poetaster.

I 'll Stay Out of Your Diet if You 'll Stay Out of Mine

I prefer charity to hospitality because charity begins
    at home but hospitality ends there,
Meaning that eventually you have to feed your
    friends there,
And you try to be both hospitable and methodical,
So you find out whose wife is currently on the
    current diet from the current fashionable
    thirty-five-cent periodical,
And it is Mrs. Pulsifer, for whom a simple cod-
    dled egg will do the job,
And you decide to feed the normal people squab,

And you wish Mrs. Pulsifer joy of her titbit to the
   ultimate dreg,
And eight diners sit down to seven squabs and a
   coddled egg,
And after two days of her three-day diet Mrs.
   Pulsifer complains of ravening pangs in her
   vestibule,
And hints wistfully that she craves solid food, be
   it never so indigestibule,
And one eye looks Goya,
And the other paranoia—
Oh, riddle me this, I beg:
What guest do you think ends up with the seventh
   squab, and what host feasts royally on
   coddled egg?

Like a Rat in a Trap

After various guesses at last I've guessed
Why in spring I feel depressed.
When the robins begin to play
Summer is just a step away.
Then hardly the summer has commenced

When autumn is what you're up against,
And once that autumn has muscled in on you
Winter is waiting to begin on you.
So spring isn't spring, but otherwise,
Just a prelude to winter, which I despise.

The Bird to the Bees

There is obviously a complete lack of understanding
    between the bee
And me.
You can't say Please
To bees.
At least, no matter with how many pleases your
    speech is bedecked,
It doesn't have any effect.
This is the simple truth that I unwilling found,
From bees following me around.
Bees cease their booming to and fro
To boom where I go;
Wherever I come,
Bees come too and hum;
Wherever I am,

There is some bee boomin' like Singin' Sam.

Night and day, day and night, under the hide of me,

There's an oh such a hungry, burning yearning
to know why bees pay so much attention to
me and upset me so and don't pay any
attention at all to or upset at all the bride
of me,

Most people who are bothered by bees are
bothered by bees only during May, June,
July, August, and the early part of September,

But any time of the year in which the busy bees do
not make me their business I cannot remember.

They are like the United States Mails, for the ele-
ments mean nothing to them,

And my garments are of what they wish to be in
the vicinity of the hem,

And there is no sanctuary indoors,

For the room has not been built which I can enter
without some bee which has been tuning up
its motor, well, suddenly into life it roars,

And roses are red and violets blue,

And that's what bees ought to eat, but whatever I
am eating they want to eat it too,

And I think that bees are what my view of life is
    owing to,
Because no bee has stung me yet but I always think
    that every bee I meet, and I meet a lot of
    bees, is going to,
And so I am ridden through life with bees in the
    saddle and stirrup,
So you take honey if you want, but I 'll take
    maple syrup.

April Yule, Daddy!

Roses are things which Christmas is not a bed of
    them,
Because it is the day when parents finally realize
    that their children will always be a jump
    ahead of them.
You stay up all night trimming the tree into a
    veritable fairyland and then in the joyous
    morn you spring it on the children in a blaze
    of glory, and who says Ooh!?
You.
And you frantically point out the dictator's ransom
    in building sets and bicycles and embarrass-

ingly lifelike dolls with which the room is
    checkered,
And the little ones pay about as much attention to
    them as they would to the punctuation in the
    Congressional Record.
Because they are fully occupied in withdrawing all
    the books from the bookcase to build a house
  · to house the pup in,
Or pulling down the curtains to dress up in,
And you stand hangdoggedly around because you
    haven't any place to go,
And after a while they look casually over at the
    dictator's ransom and say: 'Are those the
    presents? Oh.'
And you console yourself by thinking Ah happy
    apathy, as long as we haven't had an emo-
    tional climax maybe we won't have an
    emotional anticlimax, maybe we'll get
    through the day without hysterics, ah happy
    apathy,
Ah may this Yuletide indeed turn out to be the
    Yuletide without mishapathy.
Ah could this sensational lull but be permanent
    instead of pro tem.;

Ah and doubly ah, if Christmas Day could but end
    at eleven a.m.!—
But it doesn't, but the lull does, and here's some-
    thing else you discover as you keep on living,
Which is that Christmas doesn't end for about two
    weeks after Christmas, but it starts all over
    again right after the following Thanksgiving.

The Strange Case of the Wise Child

Pendleton Birdsong was a wise child.

He knew a hawk from a handsaw and a vaccina-
tion from a vacation.

He knew which side his bread was buttered on
and enough to come in out of a monsoon.

At the age of three he had mastered the principles
of higher mathematics.

When attacked by measles he spent several im-
proving hours in counting his spots and

multiplying them by the cube root of seven,
thirteen, and one hundred and twenty-nine
and one half.

He could tell any one who would listen just why
parallel lines never meet.

Or, if they do, why they do.

He knew the difference between an egoist and an
egotist and a gourmand and a gourmet and
how to make out an income tax return.

Pendleton Birdsong was a wise child.

He knew his own father.

He was all fixed.

He said he was the wise child that knew its own
father, and he was all fixed.

Senator Borah said Oh he was, was he, and how
about The child is father of the man?

You should have seen Pendleton Birdsong's face.

He said he was going home to figure it out.

He said You knew how it was about repartee, you never could think of anything to say until you got home.

Then it came over you in a flash.

Senator Borah just leered and went off to embarrass the Administration.

Pendleton Birdsong sat down to uncomplicate this complication.

He said I am the wise child that knows its own father.

Now it seems that I am also father of the man.

That means Me after I have passed through adolescence and entered maturity.

Therefore I am my own father.

26

But I know my own father, and he's not me.

Maybe I had better ask him to make sure.

He did, and he said he wasn't.

He added that brothers and sisters had he none, but Pendleton Birdsong's father was his father's son.

That didn't get anybody anywhere much.

Then Pendleton Birdsong remembered that he was not yet a man, so he could not yet be his own father.

Furthermore when he got to be a man he wouldn't be a child, and it was a child that the man was to be the son of.

Even furthermore when he got to be a man he wouldn't be a wise child, so he wouldn't know his father any more.

The child that he was now but wouldn't be when he was a man would be his father.

The father he wouldn't know any more would be himself.

So he wouldn't know himself any more.

By this time he didn't want to.

He caught measles again and read Peter Rabbit instead of counting his spots.

He attracted much unfavorable attention in the neighbourhood by trying to saw wood with a hawk.

He grew up to be a piano mover and had seventeen children.

One day they all came to him and said they knew their father.

He said he did too.

Mrs. Birdsong almost died.

Lines to a World-Famous Poet Who Failed to Complete a World-Famous Poem or Come Clean, Mr. Guest!

Oft when I 'm sitting without anything to read
    waiting for a train in a depot,
I torment myself with the poet's dictum that to
    make a house a home, livin' is what it takes
    a heap o'.
Now, I myself should very much enjoy makin' my
    house a home, but my brain keeps on a-goin'
    clickety-click, clickety-click, clickety-click,
If Peter Piper picked a peck o' heap o' livin', what
    kind of a peck o' heap o' livin' would Peter
    Piper pick?
Certainly a person doesn't need the brains of a
    Lincoln
To know that there are many kinds o' livin', just
    as there are many kinds o' dancin' or huntin'
    or fishin' or eatin' or drinkin'.
A philosophical poet should be specific
As well as prolific,
And I trust I am not being offensive
If I suggest that he should also be comprehensive.
You may if you like verify my next statement by

sending a stamped, self-addressed envelope
to either Dean Inge or Dean Gauss,
But meanwhile I ask you to believe that it takes a
heap of other things besides a heap o' livin'
to make a home out of a house.
To begin with, it takes a heap o' payin',
And you don't pay just the oncet, but agayin and
agayin and agayin.
Buyin' a stock is called speculatin' and buyin' a
house is called investin',
But the value of the stock or of the house fluc-
tuates up and down, generally down, just as
an irresponsible Destiny may destine.
Something else that your house takes a heap o',
whether the builder came from Sicily or Erin,
Is repairin',
In addition to which, gentle reader, I am sorry to
say you are little more than an imbecile or
a cretin
If you think it doesn't take a heap o' heatin',
And unless you 're spiritually allied to the little
Dutch boy who went around inspectin' dikes
lookin' for leaks to put his thumb in,
It takes a heap o' plumbin',

And if it's a house that you're hopin' to spend
    not just to-day but to-morrow in,
It takes a heap o' borrowin'.
In a word, Macushla,
There's a scad o' things that to make a house a
    home it takes not only a heap, or a peck, but
    at least a bushela.

I Happen to Know

Hark to the locusts in their shrill armadas.
Locusts aren't locusts. Locusts are cicadas.

To seals in circuses I travel on bee lines.
Seals aren't seals. Seals are sea lions.

I'm a buffalo hunter. Want to see my licence?
Buffaloes aren't buffaloes. Buffaloes are bisons.

I'm too old to be pedantically hocus-pocused.
I'll stand on the buffalo, the seal and the locust.

One of the hardest explanations to be found
Is an explanation for just standing around.
Any one just standing around looks pretty sinister,
Even a minister;
Consider then the plight of the criminal,
Who lacks even the protective coloration of a
    hyminal,
And as just standing around is any good criminal's
    practically daily stint,
I wish to proffer a hint.
Are you, sir, a masher who blushes as he loiters,
Do you stammer to passers-by that you are merely
    expecting a street car, or a dispatch from
    Reuter's?
Or perhaps you are a safe-blower engaged in casing
    a joint;
Can you look the patrolman in the eye or
    do you forget all the *savoir faire* you ever
    loint?
Suppose you are a shoplifter awaiting an oppor-
    tunity to lift a shop,
Or simply a novice with a length of lead pipe

killing time in a dark alley pending the
     arrival of a wealthy fop,
Well, should any official ask you why you are just
     standing around,
Do you wish you could simply sink into the
     ground?
My dear sir, do not be embarrassed, do not reach
     for your gun or your knife,
Remember the password, which, uttered in a tone
     of quiet despair, is the explanation of any
     one's standing around anywhere at any hour
     for any length of time: 'I'm waiting for my
     wife.'

Pride Goeth Before a Raise or *Ah, There, Mrs. Cadwallader-Smith!*

The Cadwallader-Smiths
Are People with Poise;
I consider them one of the minor joys,
Though frequently wishing
That I could share
Their imperturbable *savoir faire.*

Madame is a modishly youthful matron,
Artfully dyed and I think enameled;
Monsieur is a generous opera patron,
A Man-about-Town, by trade untrammeled.
Oh the dapper dandies,
The haughty dames,
In the phalanx of hy-
Phenated names!
(Have you ever observed
That the name of Smith
Is the oftenest hy-
Phenated with?)
In the days when they acted namby-pambily
Madame and Monsieur acquired a fambily,
Which accounts for the junior Cadwallader-Smiths,
Those perennial rotogravurian myths,
Maidens who scale the Alps and Rockies,
Debutantes with the world in tow,
Polo players and gentleman jockeys,
And athletes tailored in Savile Row.
Oh glamorous girls and golden boys,
They practically palpitate with poise!
Say me a word. It's a word they've got.
So what?

Well, though hardly copy for a great biographer,
They know how to twinkle for a news photo-
    grapher.
They don't go to work, but they wallow in shekels,
And they sit on beaches and don't get freckles.
They exchange divorces without bearing malice,
And they all get presented at Buckingham Palace.
They receive reporters with a nonchalant air,
And they 're dignified even in the barber chair,
They are dignified even in their testimonials
To beautifying lotions for the crude Colonials.
They take a paper and they read the headlines,
So they 've heard of unemployment and they 've
    heard of breadlines,
And they philanthropically cure them all
By getting up a costume charity ball.
They own a mansion in the borough of Manhattan
Which they use about as much as Greek and Latin,
And they tipple nectar and they nibble lotus,
And they pay no attention to a jury notus,
And they don't get a summons when they run past
    stoplights,
So they have the point of view of true cosmo-
    polites,

And they look you in the eye through their gold
      lorgnettes
And advise cancellation of the foreign debts.
They could all pay taxes, but they 'd rather not.
So what?

Well, they 're People with Poise,
The Cadwallader-Smiths,
With the sensitive senses of monoliths,
Which I freely admit
I could use myself,
Had I all I desire of profit and pelf.

The Panda

I love the Baby Giant Panda;
I 'd welcome one to my veranda.
I never worry, wondering maybe
Whether it isn't Giant Baby;
I leave such matters to the scientists:
The Giant Baby—and Baby Giantists.
I simply wish a julep and a
Giant Baby Giant Panda.

Do, Do, Do What You Done, Done, Done Before, Before, Before

There is a man whose name must be, I think, Mr.
    Oglethrip, and if you will bring me his head
    on a silver charger I will award you the hand
    of my daughter and a lien on my future
    salary,

And nobody has ever seen him but when you go
    to an amateur performance of any kind he is
    always sitting in the upper left-hand corner
    of the gallery,

And he has the hands of a blacksmith and a heart
    full of enthusiasm,

And compared to the rest of the audience, well Mr.
    Oglethrip is not as chusiasm,

Because seasoned amateur performance attenders
    generally weigh their applause carefully so as
    not to be either a spendthrift or a hoarder,

Because unless the performers of any performance
    are your grandmother or your favorite cousin
    or something your aim is to applaud just
    enough to not hurt their feelings and not
    enough to induce them to duplicate the order,

And some girl who once handed you a cup
of cocoa at a church supper appears and
renders an imitation of Fanny Grice imitating
Gertrude Lawrence,

And your applause preserves the delicate balance
between ecstasy and abhorrence,

And she is just about to resign the stage to the next
performer and everything is as right as a
couple of trivets,

When hark! What is that thunder in the upper
left-hand corner of the gallery, can Mr. Oglethrip be driving rivets?

No, but he is clapping his horny hands and before
you can say 'Gadzooks,'

Why, the cocoa girl is back with an imitation of
Gertrude Lawrence imitating Baby Snooks.

Mr. Oglethrip's cup has no brim,

Mr. Oglethrip is he to whom what is too
much for anybody else is never enough for
him,

If Mr. Oglethrip heard Will Hays sing 'Trees,'

He would want a reprise.

Do you know a picture program that Mr. Oglethrip
would find simply peachy?

A double bill in which each picture contained a
        dual role for Don Ameche.
I think it would be nice
If when you cut off Mr. Oglethrip's head to bring
        to me on a silver charger you would cut it
        off twice.

What, No Oysters?

There is no R in the month of May,
There's none in the month of June,
And the days of the dog, July and Aug.,
Glide past on R-less shoon.
Then where are you going, my pretty maid,
And what will you find to eat
While the oyster broods in inedible moods
In his lonely bridal suite?

'I'm going a-feasting, sir,' she said,
'I am on my way to dine.
Let the succulent bivalve cling to its bed,
Methinks I am doing fine.
For the chowder laves the fragrant clam

39

In the old New England style,
And if corn on the cob with my teeth plays hob,
I 'll remember not to smile.

'The baby lobster scarlet gleams
Next a mound of fresh asparagus;
While the blue point dreams connubial dreams,
I 'll munch till my veins are varacus.
Lo, luscious now as an infant's lisp,
The strawberry, tart and juicy,
And soft-shell crabs as sweet and crisp
As a nocturne by Debussy.

'Though there is no R in the month of May,
And none in the month of June,
Nor the days of the dog, July and Aug.,
You can stuff till you 're fit to swoon—
Who 's that a-ringing the doorbell so,
Louder than doorbell ought to ring?
Why, it 's half a dozen oysters, bowing low,
And their mouths are simply watering.'

Up, up, lad, time 's a-wastin', press the ignition.
If relief is not forthcoming, consult your physician.
Winnow your symptoms, but never discard the
    chaff,
And consult your physician, your physician de-
    serves a laugh.
Explain that when you swallow so much as a
    coddled egg it sticks like a fishbone
Somewhere behind your wishbone;
Inquire why your eyes of a sudden refuse to be
    focused,
And what is the sound in your ears like a courting
    locust.
Your physician 's a man of talents;
Ask him whatever became of your sense of balance.
Don't be irked by his suavity;
Tell how you walk with your legs braced wide
    lest you trip over gravity;
Tell him, too, that your gaze is fixed on your shoes
    as you walk, and better to tell him why:
That a too long upward glance would send you
    headlong into the sky.

Tell him straight that on such and such a day
They took the difference between down and up
away.
Give him your problem to solve,
Ask him what to hold on to when under your feet
you can feel the earth revolve;
Every molehill a mountain, every wormhole a
crater,
And every step like the step at the top of the
escalator,
And don't forget
To reveal your discovery that hair can sweat.
Go ahead, tell him;
Release the cat from the bag, let the doctor bell
him.
Give the doctor the chart, show him the map and
the graph;
If relief is not forthcoming, it says right here on
the label, consult your physician, your physi-
cian deserves a laugh.

So this is bronchitis.

Well at least it is not appendicitis.

Well I suppose I ought to be thankful it's not
bubonic or pellagra.

Well I suppose I ought to be thankful I'm having
it in bed instead of floating in a barrel over
Niagra,

And that is about all that can be said for it,

Particularly when you try to sustain life on what
you get fed for it,

And you drink water, water, water, and the only
other ingredient in it is sometimes soda and
sometimes aspirin,

And when your helpmeet approaches to help, you
are very grateful but you are afraid of giving
her what you have got, and a grateful embrace
is the last thing you can claspirin,

And if you smoke you increase your cough

But finally you decide you'd rather increase it
than lay off,

And sometimes you are cold and that's a chill and
sometimes you are hot and that's a fever

And all in all you are as merry as Danny Deever.

And if you try to read you go to sleep and if you go to sleep you are waked up by somebody advancing on your bedside without any stealth

And they poke a spoonful of something at you and tell you to swallow it and regain your health

And then you decide that if that is the only way to regain your health you just don't want to,

And then you begin to wonder who gave you your beautiful bonny bronchitis, and then finally you get to the fun of thinking who it would be fun to pass it on to,

And first of all for the good of humanity,

You'd like to give it to all dictators and political spellbinders of dubious sanity,

Because if they had bronchitis they couldn't spellbind and if they couldn't spellbind they couldn't dictate, and if they couldn't dictate they would have to stop going around with their jaws out or their right hands raised or their arms akimbo,

And they would sink back into their original limbo.

And something I should love even better than
   possums love persimmons
Would be to hand on my bronchitis to all singers
   who if they are women have voices like men's
   and if they are men have voices like women's,
And then, except for the sound of coughing, the
   day and night air would be quiet as it was
   before the birth of Marconi or Edison,
And now good-bye thank you because I must
   explain to a woman that I don't need any
   more medicine.

The Sniffle

In spite of her sniffle,
Isabel's chiffle.
Some girls with a sniffle
Would be weepy and tiffle;
They would look awful,
Like a rained-on waffle,
But Isabel's chiffle
In spite of her sniffle.
Her nose is more red
With a cold in her head,

But then, to be sure,
Her eyes are bluer.
Some girls with a snuffle,
Their tempers are uffle,
But when Isabel's snivelly
She's snivelly civilly,
And when she is snuffly
She's perfectly luffly.

The Voice of Experience

A husband at a lecture
Twitches his architecture.

He undergoes the lecturing
Like unanesthetized vivisecturing.

He's a glassy-eyed conjecturer
Of the ancestry of the lecturer.

Husbands hide in storerooms
To escape Town Halls and Forums.

They improvise In Memoriams
For speakers in auditoriums.

They regard as nauseous nostrums
Opinions delivered from rostrums.

They feel about orators' rhetorics
Like Caesar about Vercingetorix.

They flinch as the fog of boredom
Creeps verbosely toredom.

Their collars grow more and more cumbersome,
And at last they essay to slumber some.

But this respite their spouses grudge them,
And if they nod, they nudge them.

There is none so irate and awkward
As a husband being Chautauquard.

Presenting Dr. Fell

I know a man whom because he isn't a doctor I
    think of as Dr. Fell,
And I do not love him for reasons which I am
    delighted to tell.

Although he is a good citizen and a respected
    vestryman
He is unfit to be either a motorist or a pedestriman.
His is the car always approaching just as you are about
    to step off the curb, but you don't mind him,
Because you plan to cross as soon as he passes,
    because the next car is half a mile behind him,
But with your plan he plays havoc,
Because you have forgotten that he moves at the
    pace of molasses in Reykjavik,
And by the time he is gone and you are ready to
    step on the street,
Why the traffic formerly half a mile behind him
    has descended on you with the speed and
    power of a husband quashing his wife's
    suggestions for the disposition of the fleet.
Dr. Fell is he who when as a dutiful driver you
    halt for the red,
Stands on the corner with a newspaper buried in
    his head;
Until you start to start with the green;
When he steps in front of you with the carefree
    countenance of one who is beginning the be-
    guine.

Such is Dr. Fell, and I fear that I shall never be a
    friend of him
Particularly as long as he parks his car in a two-car
    space with half a space sticking out at each
    end of him.

Look What You Did, Christopher!

In fourteen hundred and ninety-two,
Somebody sailed the ocean blue.
Somebody borrowed the fare in Spain
For a business trip on the bounding main,
And to prove to people, by actual test,
You could get to the East by traveling West,
Somebody said, Sail on! Sail on!
And studied China and China's lingo,
And cried from the bow, There's China now!
And promptly bumped into San Domingo.
Somebody murmured, Oh dear, oh dear!
I've discovered the Western Hemisphere.

And that, you may think, my friends, was that.
But it wasn't. Not by a fireman's hat.

Well enough wasn't left alone,
And Columbus was only a cornerstone.
There came the Spaniards,
There came the Greeks,
There came the Pilgrims in leather breeks.
There came the Dutch,
And the Poles and Swedes,
The Persians, too,
And perhaps the Medes,
The Letts the Laps and the Lithuanians,
Regal Russians, and ripe Roumanians.
There came the French
And there came the Finns,
And the Japanese
With their friendly grins.
The Tartars came,
And the Terrible Turks—
In a word, humanity shot the works.
And the country that should have been Cathay
Decided to be
The U.S.A.

And that, you may think, my friends, was that.
But it wasn't.   Not by a fireman's hat.

Christopher C. was the cornerstone,
And well enough wasn't left alone.
For those who followed
When he was through,
They burned to discover something, too.
Somebody, bored with rural scenery,
Went to work and invented machinery,
While a couple of other mental giants
Got together
And thought up Science.
Platinum blondes
(They were once peroxide),
Peruvian bonds
And carbon monoxide,
Tax evaders
And Vitamin A,
Vice crusaders,
And tattle-tale gray—
These, with many another phobia,
We owe to that famous Twelfth of Octobia.
O misery, misery, mumble and moan!
Someone invented the telephone,
And interrupted a nation's slumbers,
Ringing wrong but similar numbers.

Someone devised the silver screen
And the intimate Hollywood magazine,
And life is a Hades
Of clicking cameras,
And foreign ladies
Behaving amorous.
Gags have erased
Amusing dialog,
As gas replaced
The cracking firelog.
All that glitters is sold as gold,
And our daily diet grows odder and odder,
And breakfast foods are dusty and cold—
It's a wise child
That knows its fodder.
Someone invented the automobile,
And good Americans took the wheel
To view American rivers and rills
And justly famous forests and hills—
But somebody equally enterprising
Had invented billboard advertising.
You linger at home
In dark despair,
And wistfully try the electric air.

You hope against hope for a quizz imperial,
And what do they give you?
A doctor serial.
Oh, Columbus was only a cornerstone,
And well enough wasn't left alone,
For the Inquisition was less tyrannical
Than the iron rules of an age mechanical,
Which, because of an error in '92,
Are clamped like corsets on me and you,
While Children of Nature we'd be to-day
If San Domingo
Had been Cathay.
And that, you may think, my friends, is that.
But it isn't—not by a fireman's hat.
The American people,
With grins jocose,
Always survive the fatal dose.
And though our systems are slightly wobbly,
We'll fool the doctor this time, probly.

No Bonds To-day

Every time you buy a bond
Adolf has a stroke.
Why annoy Adolf?
Can't you take a joke?

Every time you buy a bond
Hirohito's harried.
Wouldn't you feel guilty
If he hara-karied?

Every time you buy a bond,
There's Benito's pout.
Is anybody cad enough
To tease a stylish stout?

Every time you buy a bond
The Axites see red.
Don't irritate the Axites,
Buy a drink instead.

We Don't Need to Leave Yet, Do We? or
Yes We Do

One kind of person when catching a train always
    wants to allow an hour to cover the ten-block
    trip to the terminus,
And the other kind looks at them as if they were
    verminous,
And the second kind says that five minutes is
    plenty and will even leave one minute over
    for buying the tickets,
And the first kind looks at them as if they had
    cerebral rickets.
One kind when theater-bound sups lightly at six
    and hastens off to the play,
And indeed I know one such person who is so
    such that it frequently arrives in time for the
    last act of the matinée,
And the other kind sits down at eight to a meal
    that is positively sumptuous,
Observing cynically that an eight-thirty curtain
    never rises till eight-forty, an observation
    which is less cynical than bumptuous.
And what the first kind, sitting uncomfortably in

the waiting-room while the train is made up
in the yards, can never understand,

Is the injustice of the second kind's reaching their
seat just as the train moves out, just as they
had planned,

And what the second kind cannot understand as
they stumble over the first kind's feet just as
the footlights flash on at last

Is that the first kind doesn't feel the least bit foolish
at having entered the theater before the
cast.

Oh, the first kind always wants to start now and
the second kind always wants to tarry,

Which wouldn't make any difference, except that
each other is what they always marry.

The Smelt

Oh, why does man pursue the smelt?
It has no valuable pelt,
It boasts of no escutcheon royal,
It yields no ivory or oil,

Its life is dull, its death is tame,
A fish as humble as its name.
Yet—take this salmon somewhere else.
And bring me half a dozen smelts.

The Hat's Got My Tongue

A girl, oh a girl is a wonderful thing,
And so I am happy to say is spring,
And a girl in spring is the absolute works
But for one conspicuous item that irks:
That hat.

A girl in spring is a skylark's hymn,
An evensong in a cloister dim,
A moon in June and a dove in love,
But why the discordant detail above:
That hat?

The crocuses put their best feet foremost,
The softest, tenderest raindrops pour most,
Nature walks forth in a robe of dawn,
And you, my love, what do you put on?
That hat.

Purple the lilac and green the oaks,
Is spring the time for a milliner's hoax?
Your taste, methought, simply hibernated;
But what did I get when for spring I waited?
That hat.

A girl, oh a girl is a wonderful thing,
And so I am happy to say is spring,
And you are what I adore the sight of;
That hat is what I adore you in spite of—
Take it off and let's jump on it!

Slow Down, Mr. Ganderdonk, You're Late

Do you know Mr. Ganderdonk, he is no Einstein,
    he has no theories of Time and Space,
But he is the only man I know can be both the
    hare and the tortoise in the same race.
Mr. Ganderdonk's proclivity
Is divoty Relativity.
Put him behind you in a twosome or a foursome,
His speed is awesome.

His relationship to your rear
Is that of a catamount to a deer,
And while you are still reaching for your putter
He is standing on the edge of the green going
    mutter mutter,
But once through you in his foursome or twosome,
His torpor is gruesome.
He is a golfer that the thought of other golfers
    simply hasn't occurred to;
He has three swings for every shot, the one he
    hopes to use, the one he does use, and finally
    the one he would have preferred to.
His world from tee to cup
Consists of those behind him pressing him and
    those in front of him holding him up,
Wherefore the rest of the world is his foe
Because the rest of the world is either too fast or
    too slow.
For Mr. Ganderdonk there is only one correct pace
    and that is his,
Whatever it is.

The Common Cold

Go hang yourself, you old M.D.!
You shall no longer sneer at me.
Pick up your hat and stethoscope,
Go wash your mouth with laundry soap;
I contemplate a joy exquisite
In never paying you for your visit.
I did not call you to be told
My malady is a common cold.

By pounding brow and swollen lip;
By fever's hot and scaly grip;
By these two red redundant eyes
That weep like woeful April skies;
By racking snuffle, snort, and sniff;
By handkerchief after handkerchief;
This cold you wave away as naught
Is the damnedest cold man ever caught.

Give ear, you scientific fossil!
Here is the genuine Cold Colossal;
The Cold of which researchers dream,
The Perfect Cold, the Cold Supreme.

This honoured system humbly holds
The Supercold to end all colds;
The Cold Crusading for Democracy;
The Führer of the Streptococcracy.

Bacilli swarm within my portals
Such as were ne'er conceived by mortals,
But bred by scientists wise and hoary
In some Olympian laboratory;
Bacteria as large as mice,
With feet of fire and heads of ice
Who never interrupt for slumber
Their stamping elephantine rumba.

A common cold, forsooth, gadzooks!
Please to forgive my ribald looks,
But what derision History holds
For the man who belittled the Cold of Colds!

Creeps and Crawls

The insect world appealed to Fabre.
I find the insect world macabre.
In every hill of ants I see
A governed glimpse of what shall be,

And sense in every web contriver
Man's predecessor and survivor.
Some day, perhaps, my citronella
Will rank with Chamberlain's umbrella.

The Screen with the Face with the Voice

How long
Is a song?
O Lord,
How long?
A second?
A minute?
An hour?
A day?
A decade?
A cycle of Cathay?
Press the ears
With occlusive fingers;
The whining melody
Lingers, lingers;
The mouthing face
Will not be hid,

But leers at the eye
From the inner lid.
With the sure advance of ultimate doom
The moaning mandibles larger loom;
The seven-foot eyebrows fall and rise
In roguish rapture or sad surprise;
Eyeballs roll with fine emotion,
Like buoys rocked by a treacle ocean;
Tugged like the bell above the chapel,
Tosses the giant Adam's apple;
Oozes the voice from the magic screen,
A slow Niagara of Grenadine;
A frenzy of ripe orgiastic pain,
Niagara gurgling down a drain.
How long
Is a song?
O Lord,
How long?
As long as Loew,
And Keith,
And Albee;
It Was
And Is,
And Always Shall Be.

This is the string Time may not sever,
This is the music that lasts for ever,
This is the Womb,
This is the Tomb,
This is Alpha, Omega, and Oom!
The eyes, the eyes shall follow you!
The throat, the throat shall swallow you!
Hygienic teeth shall wolf you!
And viscous voice engulf you!
The lolloping tongue itself answer your
     question!
The Adam's apple dance at your ingestion!
And you shall never die, but live to nourish
     the bowels
Of deathless celluloid vowels.

A Visit from Dr. Fell

Dr. Fell is at the door, and I would rather have a
     visit from Herr von Ribbentrop or Count
     Ciano;
They might liquidate the family, but at least they
     wouldn't leave chocolate fingerprints in the

books and coconut-marshmallow icing on the piano.

Dr. Fell is notable for the southern-central section of his silhouette,

And he lands in your frailest chair like somebody from the ninth floor of a burning hotel landing in a net.

You know the room that used to be filled with bric-à-brac?

That's where he almost succeeded in carrying two children simultaneously pick-a-back.

Hitherto, the plumbing has functioned as sweetly as a hungry mosquito lapping up citronella,

But the plumbing is where Dr. Fell disposes of any unwanted object, from an old cigar to an old umbrella.

Dr. Fell's little finger projecting from his glass as he drinks couldn't possibly be genteeler or archer,

But whatever glasses you had a dozen of on his arrival you only have eleven of on his departure.

Every man has his own conception of enough;

Dr. Fell will not only nonchalantly knock a

half-completed jigsaw puzzle on to the floor
but nonchalantly carry off a key piece buried
in his cuff.
Come on in Dr. Fell, you must take pot-luck with
us, no, wait a minute, I forgot,
To-day we can only offer you kettle-luck, last time
you were here you ran the ice-pick through
the pot.

Here We Go Quietly Nuts in May

Do you hanker for April showers,
Or a rarefied day in June?
Give me a grade-A May day,
And please deliver it soon.
I am weary of branches naked,
Creaking like lovelorn cats;
The earth underfoot half bakèd,
And the sun overhead ersatz.
Send me a balmy zephyr
To play me a rigadoon,
And I'll gulp of my grade-A May day
Till my hiccups hammer the moon.

Have you ever spent two and a half of your three
hours' allotted shopping time hunting for a
place to park? Have you driven behind the
lady who gives you the right-turn signal and
then cuts sharp left acrows your bow? Has
the truck driver terrorized you and the road
hog sworn at you?

There is solace in the bitter whimsy of the un-
known genius who defined a thousandth of a
second as the interval between the moment
when the red light turns green and the
moment when the fellow behind starts blowing his horn at you.

But have you ever lost your early start on a six-
hundred-mile trip and had to spend the night
in an individual wayside slum instead of the
cozy inn at which you had foresightedly engaged rooms because child A couldn't find her
absolutely favorite doll, and when she did find
it, child B hadn't finished plaiting her hair yet?

Then you will agree with me that an accurate
definition of a millionth of a second is the

interval between the moment when you press
the starter as you begin a six-hundred-mile
trip and the moment when two little tired
voices inquire from the back seat: ' Are we
nearly there yet?'

Then again, consider the other millionth of a
second which lasts a year, when Time stands
still, and Eternity in the lap of Infinity lingers,

Which is while you sit in helpless paralysis while child
B carefully slams the door on child A's fingers.

Take the battle royal whose results no bachelor
need ever have computated,

Which is the struggle to sit nearest to the open
window, a struggle the prize for which is the
privilege of sticking the head and arms out in
just the right position to be immediately
omputated.

Yes, for the father of none to thank his stars I
think it only behooving,

If merely because he has not to contend with little
things who will descend from the car only
on the traffic side, and preferably quite some
time before the car but not the traffic has
stopped moving.

Yes, he can roll along as confident as brass;
No restlessly whirling little leg will knock his
spectacles off as he confronts a bus, no little
hand groping the floor for a vanilla ice cream
cone with chocolate thingamajigs on it will
suddenly alight heavily upon his gas.
As the father of two there is a respectful question
which I wish to ask of fathers of five:
How do you happen to be still alive?

Man Bites Dog-Days

In this fairly temperate clime
Summertime is itchy time.
O'er rocks and stumps and ruined walls
Shiny poison ivy crawls.
Every walk in woods and fields
Its aftermath of itching yields.
Hand me down my rusty hatchet;
Someone murmured, Do not scratch it.

Reason permeates my rhyme:
Summertime is itchy time.

Beneath the orange August moon
Overfed mosquitoes croon.
After sun-up, flies and midges
Raise on people bumps and ridges.
Hand me down my rusty hatchet;
Someone murmured, Do not scratch it.

Lo, the year is in its prime;
Summertime is itchy time.
People loll upon the beaches
Ripening like gaudy peaches.
Friends, the beach is not the orchard,
Nor is the peach by sunburn tortured.
Hand me down my rusty hatchet;
Someone murmured, Do not scratch it.

Now the menu is sublime;
Summertime is itchy time.
Berries, clams, and lobsters tease
Our individual allergies.
Rash in rosy splendor thrives,
Running neck-and-neck with hives.
Hand me down my rusty hatchet;
Someone murmured, Do not scratch it.

The bluebells and the cowbells chime;
Summertime is itchy time.
Despite cold soup, and ice, and thermoses
Garments cling to epidermises.
That fiery-footed centipede,
Prickly Heat, prowls forth to feed.
Hand me down my rusty hatchet;
Someone murmured, Do not scratch it.

Hatchet-killings ain't a crime:
Summertime is itchy time.

The Firefly

The firefly's flame
Is something for which science has no name.
I can think of nothing eerier
Than flying around with an unidentified glow on a
person's posteerier.

Tell it to the Eskimos or Tell it to the Esquimaux

Jonathan Jukes is full of health,
And he doesn't care who knows it.
Others may exercise by stealth,
But he with a cry of Prosit!
Others put up with coated tongues,
And shoulders narrow and droopy;
Jonathan overinflates his lungs
With a thundering shout of Whoopee!
Jonathan's noise is healthy noise,
Jonathan's joys are healthy joys,
Jonathan shuns the primrose path,
And starts the day with an icy bath.

I might forgive the super-physique
Contained in the Jukes apparel;
The apple glowing in either cheek;
The chest like an oyster barrel;
The muscles that flow like a mountain stream,
The result of applied eugenics;
The rigorous diet, the stern regime
Of arduous calisthenics;
I can pardon most of the healthy joys,

I can pardon most of the healthy noise,
But Heaven itself no pardon hath
For the man who boasts of an icy bath.

If the Missing Links were vigorous chaps
And their manly deeds were myriad,
Must civilization then relapse
Back to the glacial period?
Humanity learns at a fearful price;
Must the lessons all be lost?
Does the locomotive feed on ice?
Is the liner propelled by frost?

One constant truth mankind has found
Through fire and flood and slaughter:
The thing that makes the wheels go round
Is plenty of good hot water.
And therefore, therefore, Jonathan Jukes,
You deserve the harshest of harsh rebukes;
You and your frigid daily bath
Are blocking civilization's path.
You think of yourself as Spartan and spunky?
So, Jonathan, is the old brass monkey.

To My Valentine

More than a catbird hates a cat,
Or a criminal hates a clue,
Or the Axis hates the United States,
That's how much I love you.

I love you more than a duck can swim,
And more than a grape-fruit squirts,
I love you more than gin rummy is a bore,
And more than a toothache hurts.

As a shipwrecked sailor hates the sea,
Or a juggler hates a shove,
As a hostess detests unexpected guests,
That's how much you I love.

I love you more than a wasp can sting,
And more than the subway jerks,
I love you as much as a beggar needs a crutch,
And more than a hangnail irks.

I swear to you by the stars above,
And below, if such there be,
As the High Court loathes perjurious oaths,
That's how you're loved by me.

A husband is a man who two minutes after his
    head touches the pillow is snoring like an
    overloaded omnibus,
Particularly on those occasions when between the
    humidity and the mosquitoes your own bed
    is no longer a bed, but an insomnibus,
And if you turn on the light for a little reading he
    is sensitive to the faintest gleam,
But if by any chance you are asleep and he
    wakeful, he is not slow to rouse you with
    the complaint that he can't close his eyes,
    what about slipping downstairs and freez-
    ing him a cooling dish of pistachio ice
    cream.
His touch with a bottle opener is sure,
But he cannot help you get a tight dress over your
    head without catching three hooks and a
    button in your coiffure.
Nor can he so much as wash his ears without
    leaving an inch of water on the bathroom
    linoleum,
But if you mention it you evoke not a promise to

splash no more but a mood of deep melancholium.

Indeed, each time he transgresses your chance of correcting his faults grows lesser,

Because he produces either a maddeningly logical explanation or a look of martyrdom which leaves you instead of him feeling the remorse of the transgressor.

Such are husbandly foibles, but there are moments when a foible ceases to be a foible.

Next time you ask for a glass of water and when he brings it you have a needle almost threaded and instead of setting it down he stands there holding it out to you, just kick him fairly hard in the stomach, you will find it thoroughly enjoible.

The Third Jungle Book

Why does the Pygmy
Indulge in polygmy?
His tribal dogma
Frowns on monogma.

Monogma's a stigma
For any Pygma.
If he sticks to monogmy
A Pygmy 's a hogmy.

A Beginner's Guide to the Ocean

Let us now consider the ocean.
It is always in motion.
It is generally understood to be the source of
much of our rain,
And ten thousand fleets are said to have swept over
it in vain.
When the poet requested it to break break break
on its cold gray rocks it obligingly broke
broke broke.
Which as the poet was Alfred Lord Tennyson didn't
surprise him at all but if it had been me I
would probably have had a stroke.
Some people call it the Atlantic and some the
Pacific or the Antarctic or the Indian or the
Mediterranean Sea,
But I always say what difference does it make,

some old geographer mumbling a few words
of it, it will always be just the Ocean to me.
There is an immortal dignity about something
like the Atlantic,
Which seems to drive unimmortal undignified
human beings frustratedly frantic.
Just give them one foot on the beach and people
who were perfectly normal formerly, or
whilom,
Why, they are subject to whoops and capers that
would get them blackballed from an asylum;
Yet be they never so rampant and hollerant,
The ocean is tolerant,
Except a couple of times a day it gives up in disgust
and goes off by itself and hides,
And that, my dears, accounts for the tides.

Lines to be Hummed from a Supine Position to the Hummer's Osteopathic Physician

For him who botches
That delicate neck trick,
There waits, my friend,
The fauteuil electric.

Drive Slow, Man Chortling or *April*, 1941

Gangway, everybody, hold your hats,
Curb your dogs and leash your cats,
Embrace your young in parental clasp,
Breathe in deep and prepare to gasp,
Feel your pulse grow rapid and joggly,
Open your eyes and goggle agogly,
Hitch your wonderment to a star—
Here comes me in a brand-new car.

Behold this gem of automobiles!
At either end it has two wheels.
What's more, you'll notice as you draw near it
Another wheel inside, to steer it.
Oh my, how I that car admires!
The outside wheels have rubber tires.
Oh bless the day that I was born!
The inside wheel supports the horn.

My natal day I will not curse.
I've three speeds forward and one reverse.
The backward speed I truly adore,
Yet love the forward three times more.

Upon this car I am a doter;
Golly, it's even got a motor!
Nothing so much a car improves
As when you start it up, it moves.

Pour forth, my soul, in joyous hymns;
The wiper wipes, the dimmer dims,
The body on loving springs is bolstered,
And wherever you sit, it's all upholstered.
The luggage compartment is so commodious
That sleeping in it would not be odious.
Doubt if you must, but I know I'm right, there;
As a matter of fact, I spent last night there.

Oh how I pity Father Divine,
Who hasn't a new car just like mine.
Kings and emperors make mistakes
Riding around in inferior makes.
Gangway, you motoring proletariat,
Here comes me in a brand-new chariot,
And I'll sell you my thoughts for one half of
    tuppence:
A lot of road hogs are going to get their come-
    uppance.

The Duck

Behold the duck.
It does not cluck.
A cluck it lacks.
It quacks.
It is specially fond
Of a puddle or pond.
When it dines or sups,
It bottoms ups.

My Dear, How Ever Did You Think Up This Delicious Salad?

This is a very sad ballad,
Because it's about the way too many people make
 a salad.
Generally they start with bananas,
And they might just as well use gila monsters or
 iguanas.
Pineapples are another popular ingredient,
Although there is one school that holds preserved
 pears or peaches more expedient,

And you occasionally meet your fate
In the form of a prune or a date.
Rarely you may chance to discover a soggy piece
     of tomato looking very forlorn and Cin-
     derella-ry,
But for the most part you are confronted by
     apples and celery;
And it's not a bit of use at this point to turn pale
     or break out in a cold perspiration,
Because all this is only the foundation,
Because if you think the foundation sounds un-
     enticing,
Just wait until we get to the dressing, or rather,
     the icing.
There are various methods of covering up the
     body, and to some, marshmallows are the
     pall supreme.
And others prefer whipped cream,
And then they deck the grave with ground-up
     peanuts and maraschinos
And you get the effect of a funeral like Valentino's,
And about the only thing that in this kind of salad
     is never seen
Is any kind of green,

And oil and vinegar and salt and pepper are at a
   minimum,
But there is a maximum of sugar and syrup and
   ginger and nutmeg and cinnamum,
And my thoughts about this kind of salad are just
   as unutterable
As parsnips are unbutterable,
And indeed I am surprised that the perpetrators
   haven't got around to putting buttered
   parsnips in these salmagundis,
And the salad course nowadays seems to be a
   month of sundaes.

The Gander

Be careful not to cross the gander,
A bird composed of beak and dander.
His heart is filled with prideful hate
Of all the world except his mate,
And if the neighbours do not err
He's overfond of beating her.
Is she happy? What's the use
Of trying to psychoanalyze a goose?

What are friends?

Why, they are people for love of whom one goes
out and eagerly borrows what one to them
eagerly lends,

Who in return assure one that if one were about
to be eaten by an octopus they would dive
fathoms deep to the rescue at the risk of
contracting the bends,

But who, if one faces any more prosaic emergency
such as asking if they would mind one's
bringing along an extra girl, one is making a
mistake if one on them depends.

They are people on whose entertainment one's
entire income one hospitably and heb-
domadally spends,

And who at one's house eat birthright and at their
house one eats pottage and other odds and
ends,

And for whose behavior one is to one's foes
constantly making amends,

Yes, that's what are friends.

What then are foes?

Why they are the least of anybody sensible's
  woes,
Because if there is one thing that you might of
  anybody sensible suppose,
It is that he wouldn't have anything to do with
  people who prove to be foes,
Because obviously if one tarries blithely among
  one's proven foemen,
Why whom has one to blame but oneself if one
  receives a poisoned barb in the small of the
  back or a poisoned comment on the large of
  the abdomen?
Yes, friends are unavoidable and epidemic and
  therefore friend trouble is forgivable but I
  have no sympathy for him who circles Robin
  Hood's barn and exposes
Himself to foeses.
I maintain that foes are very nice people as long
  as a reasonable distance separates oneself and
  them, whereas a friend in need or in his cups
  can reach you across mountains of glass and
  lakes of fire, with which remark I shall now
  close,
Simply pausing to add that compared to a friend

at the front door I find foes at a reasonable
distance rather restful, and from now on I
shall ever think of them as *Comme Il Fauts*.

A Brief Explanation of Women

Women have antiques
In their pantiques.

Put Back Those Whiskers, I Know You

There is one fault that I must find with the
    twentieth century,
And I'll put it in a couple of words: Too adventury.
What I'd like would be some nice dull monotony
If any one's gotony.
People have gone on for years looking forward
    hopefully to the beginning of every fresh
    anno Domini,
Full of more hopes than there are grits in hominy,
Because it is their guess that the Old Year has been
    so bad that the New Year cannot help being
    an improvement, and may I say that they
    would never make a living as guessers,

Because what happens, why the New Year simply combines and elaborates on the worst features of its predecessors.

Well, I know what the matter is, it stands out as clear as a chord in a symphony of Sibelius's,

The matter is that our recent New Years haven't been New Years at all, they have just been the same Old Year, probably 1914 or something, under a lot of different aliases.

In my eagerness to encounter a New Year I stand ahead of most,

But only if it's a true New Year, not if it's merely the same Old Year with its beard shaved off and wearing a diaper labeled New Year just to get on the cover of the Saturday Evening Post,

Because there are few spectacles less convincing or more untidy

Than 1914 or something in a didy.

I am in favor of honesty as well as gluttony,

And I don't want a second-hand or repossessed January first any more than I want my spring lamb leathery and muttony.

Well anyhow, come on New Year, I may not be

able to paint as capably as Rembrandt or Dali or El Greco,

But if you are a true New Year I can shout Happy True New Year everybody! quicker than Little Sir Echo.

Good-by, Bugs

Some insects feed on rosebuds,
And others feed on carrion.
Between them they devour the earth.
Bugs are totalitarian.

No Doctors To-day, Thank You

They tell me that euphoria is the feeling of feeling wonderful, well, to-day I feel euphorian,

To-day I have the agility of a Greek god and the appetite of a Victorian.

Yes, to-day I may even go forth without my galoshes,

To-day I am a swashbuckler, would anybody like me to buckle any swashes?

This is my euphorian day,
I will ring welkins and before anybody answers I
    will run away.
I will tame me a caribou
And bedeck it with marabou.
I will pen me my memoirs.
Ah youth, youth! What euphorian days them
    was!
I wasn't much of a hand for the boudoirs,
I was generally to be found where the food was.
Does anybody want any flotsam?
I've gotsam.
Does anybody want any jetsam?
I can getsam.
I can play chopsticks on the Wurlitzer,
I can speak Portuguese like a Berlitzer.
I can don or doff my shoes without tying or un-
    tying the laces because I am wearing moc-
    casins,
And I practically know the difference between
    serums and antitoccasins.
Kind people, don't think me purse-proud, don't
    set me down as vainglorious;
I'm just a little euphorious.

Dance Unmacabre

This is the witching hour of noon;
Bedlam breaks upon us soon.
When the stroke of twelve has tolled
What a pageant doth unfold.
Drawers slam on pads of notes,
Eager fingers clutch at coats;
Compact, lipstick, comb and hat,
Here a dab and there a pat;
The vital letter just begun
Can sulk in the machine till one.
Stenographers on clicking heels
Scurry forth in quest of meals;
Secretaries arm in arm
Fill the corridors with charm;
The stolid air with scent grows heavy
As bevy scuttles after bevy;
Like the pipers on the beach,
Calling shrilly each to each,
Sure as arrows, swift as skaters,
Converging at the elevators.
From the crowded lift they scatter
Bursting still with turbulent chatter;

The revolving door in rapture whirls
Its quarters full of pretty girls,
Soignée, comme il faut and chic
On ten to seventeen a week.
When One upon the dial looms
They hurry to their office tombs,
There to bide in dust till five,
When they come again alive.

It 's a Grand Parade It Will Be, Modern Design

Saint Patrick was a proper man, a man to be
    admired;
Of numbering his virtues I am never, never tired.
A handsome man, a holy man, a man of mighty deeds,
He walked the lanes of Erin a-telling of his beads.
A-telling of his beads, he was, and spreading of the
    word.
I think that of Saint Patrick's Day, Saint Patrick
    hadn't heard.

The saint was born a subject of the ancient British
    throne,
But the Irish in their wisdom recognized him as
    their own.

A raiding party captured him, and carried him
    away,
And Patrick loved the Irish, and he lived to capture
    they,
A-walking of the valleys and a-spreading of the
    word.
I think that of Saint Patrick's Day, Saint Patrick
    hadn't heard.

He defied the mighty Druids, he spoke them bold
    and plain,
And he lit the Easter fire on the lofty hill of Shane.
He lit the Easter fire where the hill and heaven met,
And on every hill in Ireland the fire is burning yet.
He lit the Easter fire, a-spreading of the word.
I think that of Saint Patrick's Day, Saint Patrick
    hadn't heard.

Saint Patrick was a proper man before he was a
    saint,
He was shaky in his Latin, his orthography was
    quaint,
But he walked the length of Ireland, her moun-
    tains and her lakes,

A-building of his churches and a-driving out the
    snakes,
A-building of his churches and a-spreading of the
    word.
I think that of Saint Patrick's Day, Saint Patrick
    hadn't heard.

But the radio announcer is ever in the vogue;
He ushers in Saint Patrick with a rolling Broadway
    brogue,
He oils the vernal air waves with macushlas and
    colleens,
Begorras, worra-worras, and spurious spalpeens.
If Saint Francis had a sponsor, we would hear him
    as a thrush,
And Saint George would cackle cockney.
Saint Patrick, here's my blush.

Down the Mousehole, and What Science Missed There

This is a baffling and forbidding world of dis-
    reputable international shakedowns,
And reputable scientists spending their lives trying
    to give mice nervous breakdowns.

Let us treat these scientists to a constructive suggestion on the house:

Have they thought to try their experiments on a married, or at least an engaged, mouse?

This suggestion is not frivolous or yeasty;

I want to tell them about a mouse I know, his name is Roger, who loses his mind at a twist of the wrist from his fiancée, later his wife, who first caught his eye because she seemed to him naught but, as he puts it, a wee sleekit cow'rin' tim'rous beastie.

Now, it is Roger's contention that to err is mouse-like, and being only mouse, though indeed his paternal grandmother was a mountain, he is all too often conscious of having erred not only as a mouse,

But as a mouse's spouse,

As a result of which when he is justly chastised,

He is, as a reasonable mouse, neither upset nor surprised.

It 's a perfectly natural sequence, Roger says resignedly, that began with Adam and Eve in the garden:

Crime, punishment, apology, theater tickets, and eventual pardon.

What gets him down, he tells me, is when he has erred and doesn't know that he has erred,

When his conscience is clear as to thought, deed, misdeed, diet and word.

It is then, says Roger, that he is ready to pay the psychiatrist a lengthy visit,

Because he can't apologize without knowing what to apologize for, whereupon the coolness which chills him for whatever he has done that he doesn't know he has done grows all the cooler for the very reason that he has no idea what is it.

Worst of all, he adds in despair, is that while racking his brains to alight on what it can be that he erred about,

Why, he often loops an extra loop about his neck by apologizing for an error that if he hadn't apologized for it she would never have heard about.

So there you are, reputable scientists, it is in trying to recollect and expiate sins that it never knew were sins,

That is why a mouse is when it spins.

July 4, 1941—July 4, 1942

How many last year were careless boys,
And fire and thunder were their toys,
And over beach and farm and park
Their hissing rockets split the dark.
Their stars flew up like flaming birds
Of Liberty, too swift for words,
And cannon crackers wrote in smoke
The free proud thoughts they never spoke,
To-day their fireworks' eloquent glow
Is understood in Tokyo.

You Cad, Why Don't You Cringe?

'Like most knaves he was a coward at heart . . .'
    The Thirteenth Chime, by T. C. H. Jacobs, p. 94.

'Like most knaves he was a coward at heart . . .'
                            Ibid., p. 238.

If wishes were horses every panhandler would
    handle his pan while urging a fiery steed on,
And if turnips were watches they 'd make as good

eating as turnips, which in the first place are
    about as appetizing as watches to feed on,
And if most knaves were cowards at heart
Everything would be as simple as Mr. T. C. H.
    Jacobs's art.
Ah, if none but the good were brave,
How well would the bad behave!
Yes, if none but the bad were poltroons
Life for the good would be all cakes and ale and
    ice cream and macaroons,
And the world would be less hag-ridden,
And the air-waves less whatever-is-to-follow-
    Prague-ridden;
The future would be more wonderful,
And less blood and thunderful,
And very much less Nazi,
And very much more hotsy-totsy.
What a pity then that so many knaves haven't
    troubled to study their part,
Because obviously they don't realize that they are
    only cowards at heart,
And golly, what can you do with a knave
When he doesn't realize that like a coward at heart
    he is supposed to behave?

Particularly when the knave seems to be a creature
of whim,
And believes that if you have something he wants
it is you who are the knave and therefore it is
you who like all knaves are a coward at heart
and not him?
I think that Mr. T. C. H. Jacobs has a splendid
idea, but I also think it is up to him to make
the start;
I think he should follow the arrantest knave he can
find into a dark alley or a Polish corridor at
midnight and convince him first that he is a
knave and second that he is a coward at heart,
And should he happily survive,
Why he can continue until he has convinced all
other knaves alive,
And their too too solid hearts into knavish
cowardice will melt,
And life will at last become truly heavenly and
svelte.

Visitors Laugh at Locksmiths or Hospital Doors Haven't Got Locks Anyhow

Something I should like to know is, which would
    everybody rather not do:
Be well and visit an unwell friend in the hospital,
    or be unwell in the hospital and have a well
    friend visit you?
This is a discussion which I am sorry that I ever
    commenced it,
For not only does it call up old unhappy memories,
    but each choice has so much to be said
    against it.
Take the sight of a visitor trying to entertain a
    patient or a patient trying to entertain a
    visitor,
It would bring joy to the heart of the Grand
    Inquisitor.
The patient either is too ailing to talk or is panting
    to get back to the chapter where the elderly
    spinster is just about to reveal to the In-
    spector that she now thinks she can identify
    the second voice in that doom-drenched
    quarrel,

And the visitor either has never had anything to
say to the patient anyway or is wondering
how soon it would be all right to depart for
Belmont or Santa Anita or Laurel,
And besides, even if both parties have ordinarily
much to discuss and are far from conver-
sational mediocrities,
Why, the austere hygienic surroundings and the
lack of ashtrays would stunt a dialogue between Madame de Staël and Socrates,
And besides, even if anybody did get to chatting
glitteringly and gaudily,
They would soon be interrupted by the arrival of
a nurse or an orderly.
It is a fact that I must chronicle with distress
That the repartee reaches its climax when the
visitor finally spots the handle on the foot of
the bed and cranks the patient's knees up and
down and says: 'That certainly is ingenious,'
and the patient answers Yes.
How many times a day do I finger my pulse and
display my tongue to the mirror while waiting
for the decision to jell:
Whether to ignore my host of disquieting symp-

toms and have to spend my days visiting friends who have surrendered to theirs, or to surrender to my own and spend my days being visited by friends who are thereby being punished for being well.

Lament on the Eve of Parting

I shall grieve, I grieve, I am grieving.
Abel is leaving.
Abel, the wise and the clever,
Is leaving, is leaving for ever.
He goes to a wealthy tycoon
For an extra five dollars a moon,
Abel, the kind and gentle
Whose faults, if any, were minor and incidental.
North Carolina was his native heath
And the gold in his heart ran all the way up to his
    teeth.
Abel, the courtly and portly
Is departing shortly.
Never were white shoes whitened or tan shoes
    tanned
As beneath his caressing hand,

Nor the silver and glass so luminous
As beneath those fingers bituminous.
Did a faucet leak, did the furnace refuse to function?
Abel had straightened it out between breakfast and
    luncheon.
Did a fuse blow, or a bulb flicker and die like the
    flame of plum-pudding brandy?
He had always a new one handy.
Did a guest request a harpoon, a harp, a tarpaulin,
    a tarpon, a turpentine hipbath, a hymnal, let
    the guest request what he would,
Abel would either produce, or rig up something
    as good.
He could string a radio aerial
Or lay out a person for burial.
His voice dark honey dripping from an olden
    golden funnel
And his 'Suh' was as good as a 'Cunnel.'
Farewell, Abel, good-by,
You recede from my misty eye,
You have left to join your tycoon
For five more dollars a moon.
O Abel, no longer visible,
Abel, I'm misible!

People have been getting up for centuries,

They have been getting up in palaces and Pullmans
    and penitentiaries.

Yes, one fact for which every historian vouches,

Is that every morning in history began with people
    getting up off their couches.

The caveman had to get up before he could go out
    and track the brontosaurus,

Verdi had to get up before he could sit down and
    compose the Anvil Chorus,

Alexander had to get up before he could go around
    being dominant,

Even Rip Van Winkle had to get up from one sleep be-
    fore he could climb the mountain and encounter
    the sleep which has made him prominent.

Some get up energetically and some in lassitude's
    throes,

And I myself happen to love a lassitude, a bonnie
    bonnie lassitude, but be that as it may,
    however they rose, they rose.

Well, birds are descended from birds and flowers
    are descended from flowers,

And human beings are descended from generation
   after generation of ancestors who got up at
   least once every twenty-four hours,

And since birds are descended from birds they
   don't have to be forced to sing like birds,
   instead of squeaking like rats,

And since flowers are descended from flowers they
   don't have to be forced to smell like flowers,
   instead of like burning rubber or the Jersey
   flats,

But you take human beings, why their countless
   generations of ancestors who were always
   arising might just as well have spent all their
   lives on their mattresses or pallets,

Because their descendants haven't inherited any
   talent for getting up at all, no, every morning
   they have to be forced to get up either by
   their own conscience or somebody else's, or
   alarm clocks or valets.

Well, there is one obvious conclusion that I have
   always held to,

Which is that if Nature had really intended human
   beings to get up, why they would get up
   naturally and wouldn't have to be compelled to.

Geddondillo

The sharrot scudders nights in the quastron now,
The dorlim slinks undeceded in the grost,
Appetency lights the corb of the guzzard now,
The ancient beveldric is otley lost.

Treduty flees like a darbit along the drace now,
Collody lollops belutely over the slawn.
The bloodbound bitterlitch bays the ostrous
    moon now,
For yesterday's bayable majicity is flunkly gone.

Make way, make way, the preluge is scarly nonce
    now,
Make way, I say, the gronderous Demiburge comes,
His blidless veins shall ye joicily rejugulate now,
And gollify him from 'twixt his protecherous gums.

Suppose He Threw It in Your Face

Please don't anybody ask me to decide anything,
    I do not know a nut from a meg,
Or which came first, the lady or the tiger, or
    which came next, the chicken or the egg.

It takes a man of vision
To make a decision,
And my every memory
Is far too dilemmary.
I am, alas, to be reckoned
With the shortstop who can't decide whether to
throw to first or second,
Nor can I decide whether to put, except after c,
E before i, or i before e.
But where this twilight mind really goes into
eclipse
Is in the matter of tips.
I stand stricken before the triple doom,
Whether, and How Much, and Whom.
Tell me, which is more unpleasant,
The look from him who is superior to a tip and
gets it, or from him who isn't and doesn't?
I had rather be discovered playing with my toes in
the Boston Aquarium
Than decide wrongly about an honorarium.
Oh, to dwell for ever amid Utopian scenery
Where hotels and restaurants and service stations
are operated by untippable unoffendable
machinery.

The Strange Case of the Irksome Prude

Once upon a time there was a young man named
    Harold Scrutiny.

Harold had many virtues and practically no vices.

He smoked, to be sure.

Also he drank and swore.

Moreover, he was a pickpocket.

But, for all that, Harold was no prude.

I am no prude, Harold often said.

But Detective Guilfoyle of the Pickpocket Squad is
    a prude, the old prude, said Harold.

One day Harold went into the subway to pick
    some pockets.

There was a man on the platform penciling a
    beard on the lady on the toothpaste placard.

Hey, said Harold.

Hey who, said the man.

Hey you, that's hey who, said Harold.

Aren't you going to give her a mustache?

Sure I'm going to give her a mustache, said the man.

What do you think I am?

I think you're somebody that puts the beard on ladies on toothpaste placards before they put on the mustache, said Harold.

Don't you know enough to put the mustache on first?

You put the mustache on first, why then you can turn it up or turn it down, whichever you want, said Harold.

You try to turn a mustache down after the beard's on, it runs into the beard, said Harold.

It don't look like a mustache, only like a beard grows up and down both.

Go on, said the man, go on and pick some pockets.

Harold turned to his work, but his mind was elsewhere.

Suddenly the lady on the toothpaste placard got off the toothpaste placard and arrested him.

It was Detective Guilfoyle of the Pickpocket Squad all the time.

You got a beard grows up and down both, said Harold.

Detective Guilfoyle searched Harold.

He certainly was surprised at what he found.

So was Harold.

Harold hadn't picked any pockets at all because his mind was elsewhere.

He had picked a peck of pickled peppers.

Detective Guilfoyle wanted to call Harold a name,
　　but he couldn't because he was a prude.

Harold picked his pocket and later became the
　　smokingest, swearingest, drinkingest Assis-
　　tant District Attorney the county ever had.

Don't be a prude.

Who Shall I Say Is Calling?

Once there was a man named Mr. Deronda James
And he gave over his life to names.
It began one day when he sipped first half a beer
　　and later an entire beer,
And a drinking companion told him the difference
　　between Biedermeier and Meyerbeer,
And he considered it an omen
And he got interested in everybody's cognomen.
The day he discovered that the Barrymores' name
　　was really Blythe,

Why you could have knocked him down with a
    scythe,
And he would positively purr
As he traced Joan Crawford back to Lucille le Sueur.
He made a new will cutting a canary hospital off
    with a dollar and leaving everything else to
    his kith
Because a second cousin told him about Mary
    Pickford and Gladys Smith,
And if anybody mentioned Robert Taylor he would
    superciliously murmur: ' Who?
I suppose you are referring to Spangler Arlington
    Brugh.'
Success was to Mr. James a dangerous drug;
I am afraid he grew a trifle smug.
Poor Mr. James, you remember how his clothes
    were found on the banks of the Rappahannock.
That was half an hour after a spiteful canary finally
    convinced him that Darryl Zanuck's name is
    Darryl Zanuck.

The Grackle

The grackle's voice is less than mellow,
His heart is black, his eye is yellow,
He bullies more attractive birds
With hoodlum deeds and vulgar words,
And should a human interfere,
Attacks that human in the rear.
I cannot help but deem the grackle
An ornithological debacle.

The Mind of Professor Primrose

My story begins in the town of Cambridge, Mass.,
Home of the Harvard Business and Dental Schools,
And more or less the home of Harvard College.
Now, Harvard is a cultural institution,
Squandering many a dollar upon professors,
As a glance at a Harvard football team makes
    obvious;
Professors wise and prowling in search of wisdom,
And every mother's son of them absent-minded.
But the absentest mind belonged to Professor
    Primrose.

He had won a Nobel award and a Pulitzer Prize,
A Guggenheim and a leg on the Davis Cup,
But he couldn't remember to shave both sides of
   his face.
He discharged the dog and took the cook for an
   airing;
He frequently lit his hair and combed his cigar;
He set a trap for the baby and dandled the mice;
He wound up his key and opened the door with
   his watch;
He tipped his students and flunked the traffic
   policeman;
He fed the mosquitoes crumbs and slapped at the
   robins;
He always said his prayers when he entered the
   theater,
And left the church for a smoke between the acts;
He mixed the exterminator man a cocktail
And told his guests to go way, he had no bugs;
He rode the streets on a bicycle built for two,
And he never discovered he wasn't teaching at Yale.
At last one summer he kissed his crimson flannels
And packed his wife in camphor, and she com-
   plained.

She had always hated camphor, and she complained.
'My dear,' she ordered, 'these *contretemps* must cease;
You must bring this absent mind a little bit nearer;
You must tidy up that disorderly cerebellum;
You must write to-day and enroll in the Pelman Institute.'
He embraced his pen and he took his wife in hand,
He wrinkled a stamp and thoughtfully licked his brow,
He wrote the letter and mailed it, and what do you know?
In a couple of days he disappeared from Cambridge.
'For heaven's sake, my husband has disappeared,'
Said Mrs. Primrose. 'Now isn't that just like him?'
And she cut the meat and grocery orders in half,
And moved the chairs in the living room around,
And settled down to a little solid comfort.
She had a marvelous time for seven years,
At the end of which she took a train to Chicago.
She liked to go to Chicago once in a while
Because of a sister-in-law who lived in Cambridge.

Her eye was caught at Schenectady by the porter;
She noticed that he was brushing off a dime,
And trying to put the passenger in his pocket.
'Porter,' she said, 'aren't you Professor Primrose?
Aren't you my husband, the missing Professor
    Primrose?
And what did you learn at the Pelman Institute?'
'Mah Lawd, Maria,' the porter said, 'mah Lawd!
Did you say *Pelman*? Ah wrote to de *Pullman*
    folks!'

Now You See It, Now I Don't

Some people look to the future and others look
    days of yore-wards,
But even they see more eye to eye than two people
    on a train one of whom is riding backwards
    and the other forwards.
I don't know how it does or when,
But anything interesting described by a forwards
    rider has vanished by the time it should have
    swum into the backwards rider's ken,
While, through a freak twist of the current,

The backwards rider gets to see a lot of interesting
things that should have been there a moment
ago for the forwards rider to see but somehow they just wurrent.
Travelers have told me and I have believed them,
That such noticeable objects as the Mississippi
River and the Sierra Nevada mountains have
disappeared between the time when the for-
wards rider pointed them out and the back-
wards rider should have perceived them.
There are those who in an effort to explain this
phenomenon have developed a disturbing
knack;
They sit forwards and look back,
While others to whom their vertebrae are dearer
Sit backwards and gaze on the fleeting landscape
through a mirror.
But no matter what they describe
Their accounts never jibe.
When I eventually establish my Universal Travel
Service and Guide Ways
I shall advise all my clients who really want to see
anything just to sit at home and look sideways.

Everybody Eats Too Much Anyhow

You gulp your breakfast and glance at the clock,
Through eleventh-hour packing you gallop amok,
You bundle your bags in the back of the car,
You enter, she enters, and there you are.
You clutch the wheel, she clutches the maps,
And longs for a couple of extra laps.
It 's *au revoir* to your modest abode,
You 're gypsies, away on the open road;
Into the highway you burst like a comet or
Heat waves climbing a Kansas thermometer.
The conversation is sweet as clover,
With breakfast practically hardly over.
' Darling, light me a cigarette? '
' At once and with all my heart, my pet;
And by the way, we are off the track;
We should have turned left a half-mile back.'
You swing around with a cheery smile,
Thus far, a mile is only a mile.
The road is romance, so let it wind,
With breakfast an hour or so behind.
Under the tires the pebbles crunch,
And through the dust creep thoughts of lunch.

The speedometer sits on a steady fifty
And more and more does lunch seem nifty.
Your eyes to the road ahead are glued,
She glances about in search of food.
She sees a place. She would like to try it.
She says so. Well, you 're already by it.
Ignoring the road, you spot an eatery;
The look of it makes her interior teetery.
She sees a beauty. You 're past it again.
Her eyebrows look like ten past ten;
She 's simmering now, and so are you,
And your brows register ten to two.
She snubs the excuse as you begin it:
That there 'll be another one any minute,
She says there won't. It must be a plot;
She 's absolutely correct. There 's not.
You finally find one. You stop and alight.
You 're both too annoyed to eat a bite.
Oh, this is the gist of my gypsy song:
Next time carry your lunch along.

The Big Tent Under the Roof

Noises new to sea and land
Issue from the circus band.
Each musician looks like mumps
From blowing umpah umpah umps.

Lovely girls in spangled pants
Ride on gilded elephants.
Elephants are useful friends,
They have handles on both ends;
They hold each other's hindmost handles
And flee from mice and Roman candles.
Their hearts are gold, their hides are emery,
And they have a most tenacious memory.

Notice also, girls and boys,
The circus horses' avoirdupois.
Far and wide the wily scouts
Seek these snow-white stylish stouts.
Calmer steeds were never found
Unattached to a merry-go-round.
Equestriennes prefer to jump
On to horses pillow-plump.

Equestriennes will never ride
As other people do, astride.
They like to balance on one foot,
And wherever they get, they won't stay put.
They utter frequent whoops and yips,
And have the most amazing hips.
Pink seems to be their favorite color,
And very few things are very much duller.

Yet I for one am more than willing
That everything should be less thrilling.
My heart and lungs both bound and balk
When high-wire walkers start to walk.
They ought to perish, yet they don't;
Some fear they will, some fear they won't.

I lack the adjectives, verbs and nouns
To do full justice to the clowns.
Their hearts are constantly breaking, I fear,
And who am I to interfere?

Still, I could interfere for weeks
With those who come to mock the freaks.

Buzzards that gloat on Nature's denials
Buy souvenirs at murder trials.

Am I making an acorn out of a quercus?
Guess again, please. Let's go to the circus!

So That's Who I Remind Me of

When I consider men of golden talents,
I'm delighted, in my introverted way,
To discover, as I'm drawing up the balance,
How much we have in common, I and they.

Like Burns, I have a weakness for the bottle,
Like Shakespeare, little Latin and less Greek;
I bite my finger nails, like Aristotle;
Like Thackeray, I have a snobbish streak.

I'm afflicted with the vanity of Byron,
I've inherited the spitefulness of Pope;
Like Petrarch, I'm a sucker for a siren,
Like Milton, I've a tendency to mope.

My spelling is suggestive of a Chaucer;
Like Johnson, well, I do not wish to die
(I also drink my coffee from the saucer);
And if Goldsmith was a parrot, so am I.

Like Villon, I have debits by the carload,
Like Swinburne, I'm afraid I need a nurse;
By my dicing is Christopher out-Marlowed,
And I dream as much as Coleridge, only worse.

In comparison with men of golden talents,
I am all a man of talent ought to be;
I resemble every genius in his vice, however
    henious—
Yet I write so much like me.

There's Always an Ubblebub

There are some fiestas that the moment you arrive
    at them you realize this is not your night to
    howl,
Because your hostess is still patting sofa cushions
    in the parlour and your host is upstairs apply-
    ing the styptic pencil to his jowl,

And you apologize for being premature,

And when your hostess snarls ' Oh that 's all right,'
    she is lying in her teeth, you may be sure,

And you wish she would keep on patting cushions
    and let you go out and walk around the
    block,

But she just sits there asking how you like their
    city and looking at the clock,

And at last in comes another guest whose name
    sounds like Miss Ubblebub, which seems
    highly improbable,

And she is wearing a dress that she wore first as a
    bridesmaid during the Harding administration
    and hair that hesitates between the waveable
    and the bobbable,

And you may not have suspected your hostess of
    craft,

But suddenly she is superintending appetizers and
    you and Miss Ubblebub are off in a corner
    as snug as two barnacles on a raft,

And an hour later when the last guest has been
    cocktailed and canapéed you have certainly
    run, as far as Miss Ubblebub is concerned,
    your conversational gamut,

And when at dinner you find yourself seated next
to Miss Ubblebub, I think you may be
excused an ardent shucks, or even a quiet
damut.

Please Pass the Biscuit

I have a little dog,
Her name is Spangle.
And when she eats
I think she 'll strangle.

She 's darker than Hamlet,
Lighter than Porgy;
Her heart is gold,
Her odor, dorgy.

Her claws click-click
Across the floor,
Her nose is always
Against a door.

The squirrel flies
Her pursuing mouth;
Should he fly north,
She pursues him south.

Yet do not mock her
As she hunts;
Remember, she caught
A milkman once.

Like liquid gems
Her eyes burn clearly;
She 's five years old,
And house-trained, nearly.

Her shame is deep
When she has erred;
She dreads the blow
Less than the word.

I marvel that such
Small ribs as these
Can cage such vast
Desire to please.

She 's as much a part
Of the house as the mortgage;
Spangle, I wish you
A ripe old dortgage.

Say About Seven or Seven-Fifteen

A supper party is something at which you arrive
    either long before or long after the rest of
    the competitors,
And you broke your glasses on the way over and
    can't tell people you know from people you
    don't know or your creditors from your
    debtitors,
And you had thought your morning shave would
    see you through and you suddenly realize
    that your chin is growing shadowy, not to
    say tufty,
And you discover that you are either the only
    male in evening clothes or the only one in
    mufti,
And as if your spirits were not by now sufficiently
    dankish,
Well, you also discover that you alone didn't
    know it was a birthday party and are the only
    arrival not to bring in a package either useful
    or prankish,
But with the arrival of the cocktails your spirits
    are turned from the swath and scattered for

drying, or as the crossword puzzlers put it, tedded,

Until you realize with a shudder that you received through an error the cocktail specially mixed by the host for his brother-in-law, who is notoriously light-headed,

And you choke it down, and not till the salad is served do you recover from your croup,

At which point it seems that you have no fork left, the implication being either that it now rests in your pocket or that you used two forks on your soup.

But it is only later that the earth really begins to spin like a fretful midge,

When it transpires that in this gathering of eight or twelve or sixteen it is you and you alone by yourself who do not play bridge.

You may well echo the words of the poet as you eventually wend your homeward way.

'Fate,' said the poet firmly, 'cannot harm me further, I have dined to-day.'

Midsummer Warning

August is sunburn and moonlight,
August 's a menace to men;
When the casual canoer discovers l'*amouer*,
August has done it again.
August is moonlight and sunburn,
When the bachelor sows as he reaps;
His sunburn will finally unburn,
But he 's burned in the moonlight for keeps.

' To-morrow, Partly Cloudy '

Rainy vacations
Try people's patience.
To expect rain in the autumn
Experience has tautumn,
And rain in the spring and winter
Makes no stories for the printer,
But rain on summer colonies
Breeds misdemeanors and felonies.
Summer cottages are meant just to sleep in,
Not to huddle all day in a heap in,

And whether at sea level or in higher places
There are not enough fireplaces,
And the bookcase stares at you starkly
And seems to be full of nothing but Volume II of
    the life of Rutherford B. Hayes, and The
    Rosary, by Florence M. Barclay,
And everybody wishes they had brought woolens
    and tweeds instead of linens and foulards,
And if you succeed in lining up four for bridge the
    only deck turns out to have only fifty-one
    cards,
And tennis rackets grow frazzled and golf sticks
    rusty and bathing suits moldy,
And parents grow scoldy,
And on all sides you hear nothing but raindrops
    going sputter-sput, sputter-sput,
And bureau drawers won't open and bathroom
    doors won't shut,
And all attempts at amusement fail,
Even reading the previous tenants' jettisoned
    mail,
Although naturally it would never have been
    jettisoned
If it hadn't been reticent.

But you could stand everything if it wasn't for
    one malignant committee,
Which is the one that turns the sun on again just
    as you are leaving for the city.
Yes indeed, rainy vacations
Certainly try people's patience.

Dr. Fell and Points West

Your train leaves at eleven-forty-five and it is now
    but eleven-thirty-nine and a half,
And there is only one man ahead of you at the
    ticket window so you have plenty of time,
    haven't you, well I hope you enjoy a hearty
    laugh,
Because he is Dr. Fell, and he is engaged in an
    intricate maneuver,
He wants to go to Sioux City with stop-overs at
    Plymouth Rock, Stone Mountain, Yellow-
    stone Park, Lake Louise and Vancouver,
And he would like some information about an
    alternate route,
One that would include New Orleans and Detroit,

with possibly a day or two in Minneapolis and Butte,

And when the agent has compiled the data with the aid of a slug of aromatic spirits and a moist bandanna,

He says that settles it, he'll spend his vacation canoeing up and down the Susquehanna,

And oh yes, which way is the bus terminal and what's playing at the Rivoli,

And how do the railroads expect to stay in business when their employees are incapable of answering a simple question accurately or civilly?

He then demands and receives change for twenty dollars and saunters off leaving everybody's jaw with a sag on it,

And when you finally get to buy your ticket not only has your train gone but you also discover that your porter has efficiently managed to get your bag on it.

Lines on Facing Forty

I have a bone to pick with Fate.
Come here and tell me, girlie,
Do you think my mind is maturing late,
Or simply rotted early?

One Night in Oz

O She whom I cannot abide,
Our hostess sat us side by side,
But must the heavy silence scream
Our heartfelt mutual disesteem?
Can we not mitigate our plight
If you turn left and I turn right?
This tasty fare will tastier taste
If by each other we are not faced;
Why shouldn't our acquaintance end,
Friend of a friend of a friend of a friend?
You do not love my way of life,
Myself, my children or my wife,
And too self-satisfied for tact,
Don't bother to conceal the fact,

While I my feelings may not hint
Till I can set them forth in print.
Our juxtaposition as we dine
Results from no intrigue of mine.
You 'd wished yon titled refugee
Whose dollars Clippered here with he,
While I, whose hopes are mild and mere,
Had but desired to not be here.
Discovering who sits next to who,
Your face fell one inch, mine fell two.
Yet o'er our hostess's well-meant food
Did I refrain from being rude,
A minor courtesy which I grieve
To note that you could not achieve.
Well, Madam, if you wish it so,
Hitch up your girdle, here we go.
O living sneer, poor painted peril,
Yours is the snobbery of the sterile.
Three husbands have you unbeguiled,
And here you stand without a child.
Of hounds and huntin' you discourse
Who never sat upon a horse.
You, who have never penned a line
That would not shame a Bantu of nine,

Serve up the great as chummy nicknames
And little intimate make-you-sick names.
How glibly in your talk you glue
Bohemia to Park Avenue,
Unwitting that your gossipy speech
Stamps you a hanger-on in each.
Ah, let us our acquaintance end,
Friend of Hemingway's friend's friend's friend;
I'm just as glad as glad can be
To feel towards you as you towards me.

The Strange Case of Mr. Fortague's Disappointment

Once upon a time there was a man named Mr.
Lionel Fortague.

He didn't have very much to talk about.

In summer he used to ask people if it was hot
enough for them.

It always was.

In winter he used to ask people if it was cold
enough for them.

It always was.

Mr. Lionel Fortague got pretty sick of people it was hot enough for.

He got pretty sick of people it was cold enough for, too.

He decided he would arise and go now.

He decided he would go to Innisfree.

The people of Innisfree are different, thought Mr. Lionel Fortague.

As soon as he got to Innisfree he asked the people if it was cold enough for them.

They asked him What? Was what cold enough for who?

Mr. Lionel Fortague was delighted.

I knew Innisfree would be different, he said to himself.

He could hardly wait for summer to verify his conclusion.

As soon as summer came he asked everybody if it was hot enough for them.

Everybody said the question was familiar but they couldn't remember the answer.

Mr. Lionel Fortague said he would settle down on Innisfree, the home of iridescent chitchat.

He said he would a small cabin build there, of clay and wattles made.

Everybody said Did he mean he would build a small cabin there, made of clay and wattles?

Mr. Lionel Fortague said yes, but his way of putting it was more poetic.

Everybody said Maybe, but they were all out of wattles.

Mr. Lionel Fortague grew very angry at the people
of Innisfree.

He a small cabin built there, of clay and beaver-
board made.

He a fierce-looking dog at an annual clearance sale
bought, and it the people of Innisfree one by
one to bite he instructed.

My, he was disappointed.

He had forgotten that a bargain dog never bites.

Thoughts Thought on an Avenue

There would be far less masculine gaming and
boozing
But for the feminine approach to feminine
fashions, which is distinctly confusing.
Please correct me if, although I don't think I do,
I err;
But it is a fact that a lady wants to be dressed

exactly like everybody else but she gets pretty
upset if she sees anybody else dressed exactly
like her.

Nothing so infuriates her as a similar hat or dress,

Especially if bought for less,

Which brings up another point which I will
attempt to discuss in my guttural masculine
jargon;

Her ideal raiment is costlier than her or her
dearest friend's purse can buy, and at the
same time her own exclusive and amazing
bargain.

Psychologists claim that men are the dreamers and
women are the realists,

But to my mind women are the starriest-eyed of
idealists,

Though I am willing to withdraw this charge and
gladly eat it uncomplaineously

If any one can explain to me how a person can
wear a costume that is different from other
people's and the same as other people's, and
more expensive than other people's and
cheaper than other people's, simultaneously.

Mr. Henderson

There goes Leon
Glowing like neon.
He's got an appointment
In somebody's ointment.

Thoughts Thought while Waiting for a Pronouncement from
   a Doctor, an Editor, a Big Executive, the Department of
   Internal Revenue or Any Other Momentous Pronouncer

Is Time on my hands? Yes it is, it is on my
      hands and my face and my torso and my
      tendons of Achilles,
And frankly, it gives me the willies.
The quarter-hour grows to the half-hour as chime
      clings to the tail of the proceding chime,
And I am tarred and feathered with Time.
No matter how frantically I shake my hands the
      hours will not drop off or evaporate,
Nor will even the once insignificant minutes
      co-operate.
The clock has stopped at Now, there is no Past, no
      Future, and oddly enough also no Now,

Only the hot, moist beaded seconds on the brow,
Only the days and nights in a gluey lump,
And the smothering weeks that stick like a swarm
    of bees to a stump.
Time stands still, or it moves forward or back-
    ward, or at least it exists, for Ex-Senator Rush
    Holt, for Doctor Dafoe, for Simon and
    Schuster, yes, and for Schiaparelli,
But for me it is limbo akimbo, an inverted void,
    a mouse with its tail pulled out of its mouth
    through its belly.
O, the world's most honored watch, I haven't
    been there, I 've been here,
For how long, for one small seventeen-jeweled
    tick, or have I been sitting a year?
I 'm a speck in infinite space,
Entombed behind my face.
Shall I suddenly start to gyrate, to rotate, to
    spiral, to expand through nebular process
    to a new universe maybe, or maybe only a
    galaxy?
But such a Goldbergian scheme to extinguish
    one lonely identity seems, well, under-
    simplified and, if I may say so, smart-alexy.

Oh, I shall arise and go now, preferably in a
     purple-and-gold palanquin,
Borne on the copper shoulders of a Seminole, an
     Apache, a Crow and an Algonquin,
And whatever be my heart's desire, be it a new
     understanding of Time or a cup of dew
     gathered from the spring's first jonquil,
Why if none of the other three will bring it to me,
     why perhaps the Algonquil.

Samson Agonistes

I test my bath before I sit,
And I'm always moved to wonderment
That what chills the finger not a bit
Is so frigid upon the fundament.

Seeing Eye to Eye Is Believing

When speaking of people and their beliefs I wear
     my belief on my sleeve;
I believe that people believe what they believe
     they believe.

When people reject a truth or an untruth it is not
     because it is a truth or an untruth that they
     reject it,
No, if it isn't in accord with their beliefs in the
     first place they simply say, 'Nothing doing,'
     and refuse to inspect it.
Likewise when they embrace a truth or an untruth
     it is not for either its truth or its mendacity,
But simply because they have believed it all along
     and therefore regard the embrace as a tribute
     to their own fair-mindedness and sagacity.
These are enlightened days in which you can get
     hot water and cold water out of the same
     spigot,
And everybody has something about which they
     are proud to be broad-minded but they also
     have other things about which you would be
     wasting your breath if you tried to convince
     them that they were a bigot,
And I have no desire to get ugly,
But I cannot help mentioning that the door of a
     bigoted mind opens outwards so that the
     only result of the pressure of facts upon it is
     to close it more snugly.

Naturally I am not pointing a finger at me,
But I must admit that I find Mr. Ickes or any other
    speaker far more convincing when I agree
    with him than when I disagree.

No, No, November

Thirty days November hath,
Unfit for human living,
Including one Election Day,
And a hide-and-seek Thanksgiving.
An encouraging month November is
For burglary and mayhem;
It 's night for most of the afternoon,
And p.m. most of the a.m.
There may be virtues in November,
But if there are I can't remember.

The Strange Case of Mr. Niobob's Transmogrification

Listen motorists, and learn:
Once there was a motorist named Mr. Niobob who
    took a trip from which he didn't return.
His first five miles were simply seraphic

Because he was on a dual highway and there
wasn't even a smattering of traffic
But then he had to leave the dual highway because
his destination was merely New York,
And dual highways never go to anybody's desti-
nation, they all lead to a deserted traffic
circle in Yoakum Corners or Medicine
Fork,
So Mr. Niobob turned off the trafficless dual highway and with his usual luck,
Well yes, he immediately found himself behind a
truck,
And whenever to pass it he mustered his nerve
Well, naturally, they came to a curve,
And it also bored him
That whenever the road straightened out and he
edged over for a dash there would be another
truck clattering toward him,
And he wished he had picked up a little voodoo on
his cruise to Haiti,
Because while the truck bogged down to three
miles per hour on the way uphill, why when
he thought to overtake it on the way down it
accelerated to eighty,

And all of a sudden they again entered a dual
    highway,
And Mr. Niobob said: 'By gum, now I can drive
    my way,'
And he stepped on the gas with all his might,
And just as he overtook the truck it turned down
    a side road on the right.
Poor frustrated Mr. Niobob, his mind slipped
    quietly over the brink,
He just sat down and cried and cried until a kind
    Commissioner of Motor Vehicles took pity on
    him and transformed him into a fountain, at
    which tired truck drivers often pause to drink.

On Gratitude We Stand Patitude

This is the Lackadaisical Broadcasting Company,
    the Friendly Voice that also stands and waits,
Bringing you our annual Thanksgiving message
    through the courtesy of the President and
    merchants of the United States.
Let us now give thanks for the happy circum-
    stances that led to the friendship of Mr. Sears

with Mr. Roebuck and Mr. Montgomery with Mr. Ward, to say nothing of the concatenation of Messrs. Barton, Durstine and Osborn and Mr. Batten,

And for not being in a bewildered state on the Jamaica platform of the Long Island Railroad and about to step into the train bound for Atlantic Avenue, Brooklyn, instead of the Pennsylvania Station, Manhattan.

Let us give thanks that women's wedge shoes weren't invented until they were,

And that the bad manners of the younger generation help middle-aged people to grow old without self-consciousness because they no longer shock you into a realization of your advanced age by offering you their chair and calling you Sir.

Yes, and let us consider that even if a lot of barytones sing 'The Road to Mandalay' and 'Danny Deever' at least very few of them sing 'Gunga Din,'

And that a batter hitting a long fly with a man on third no longer gets credit for a sacrifice but only for a run batted in.

Let us also remember with affection the confused
  Democratic delegate who spoke into the Chi-
  cago microphone saying: I want to thank the
  Chair for its recognichigan of the State of
  Michigan.'
He was indeed an engaging politichigan.
So the Lackadaisical Broadcasting Co. bids you
  farewell with the message that if you aren't
  grateful to be living in a world where so
  many things to be grateful for are yours as a
  matter of course
Why it is now five seconds until fifteen minutes
  before eleven o'clock and you are just an old
  Trojan horse.

Confessions of a Born Spectator

One infant grows up and becomes a jockey,
Another plays basketball or hockey.
This one the prize ring hastes to enter,
That one becomes a tackle or center.
I'm just as glad as glad can be
That I'm not them, that they're not me.

With all my heart do I admire
Athletes who sweat for fun or hire,
Who take the field in gaudy pomp
And maim each other as they romp;
My limp and bashful spirit feeds
On other people's heroic deeds.

Now A runs ninety yards to score;
B knocks the champion to the floor;
C, risking vertebrae and spine,
Lashes his steed across the line.
You 'd think my ego it would please
To swap positions with one of these.

Well, ego might be pleased enough,
But zealous athletes play so rough;
They do not ever, in their dealings,
Consider one another's feelings.
I 'm glad that when my struggle begins
'Twixt prudence and ego, prudence wins.

When swollen eye meets gnarlèd fist,
When snaps the knee, and cracks the wrist,
When calm officialdom demands,
Is there a doctor in the stands?

My soul in true thanksgiving speaks
For this most modest of physiques.

Athletes, I'll drink to you or eat with you,
Or anything except compete with you;
Buy tickets worth their weight in radium
To watch you gambol in a stadium,
And reassure myself anew
That you're not me and I'm not you.

For Dr. Warren *Adams*, *Who Kindly Bound the Author*
Far Beyond His Deserts

I'm prideful to the point of sin
About my new and handsome skin.
How can a Muse resist when wooed
By one so tastefully tattooed?

And Three Hundred and Sixty-Six in Leap Year

Some people shave before bathing,
And about people who bathe before shaving they
are scathing,

F 149

While those who bathe before shaving,
Well, they imply that those who shave before
    bathing are misbehaving.
Suppose you shave before bathing, well the ad-
    vantage is that you don't have to make a
    special job of washing the lather off after-
    wards, it just floats off with the rest of your
    accumulations in the tub,
But the disadvantage is that before bathing your
    skin is hard and dry and your beard confronts
    the razor like a grizzly bear defending its cub.
Well then, suppose you bathe before shaving, well
    the advantage is that after bathing your skin
    is soft and moist, and your beard positively
    begs for the blade,
But the disadvantage is that to get the lather off
    you have to wash your face all over again at
    the basin almost immediately after washing it
    in the tub, which is a duplication of effort
    that leaves me spotless but dismayed.
The referee reports, gentlemen, that Fate has
    loaded the dice,
Since your only choice is between walking around all
    day with a sore chin or washing your face twice,

So I will now go and get a shave from a smug
    man in a crisp white coat,
And I will disrupt his smugness by asking him
    about his private life, does he bathe before
    shaving or shave before bathing, and then
    I will die either of laughing or of a clean cut
    throat.

Electra Becomes Morbid

I

Abandon for a moment, friends,
Your frivolous means, your futile ends;
Life is not wholly beer and skittles,
A treasure hunt for love and victuals;
And so at times I think we ought
To pause and think a sobering thought.
Myself, I feel a dark despair
When I consider human hair.
I'm chicken-hearted, beetle-browed,
As I behold the heedless crowd,
Knowing each carefree individual
The slave of hair that runs on schidual.

On every human head or chin
It's falling out or growing in.
Yon whistling adolescent scholar,
Released from Ye Olde Tonsorial Parlor,
Runs up his neck with fingers tense
Like sticks along a picket fence.
His scalp is all Bay Rum and bristles,
Therefore he's pleased and therefore whistles.
Yea, he rejoices, quite unknowing
That all the time his hair is growing.
O woe is you, unhappy scholar,
Next month you'll be back in the tonsorial
     parlor.

II

Myself I feel a dark despair,
When I consider human hair
(Fine filaments sprouting from the skin),
I tremble like an aspirin.
For men and women everywhere
Unconsciously are growing hair,
Or, if the other hand you choose,
With every breath a hair they lose.

Unbid it cometh, likewise goeth,
And oftentimes it 's doing boeth.
This habit is the chief determinant
Why permanent waves are less than permanent.
You rise, Madame, you face your mirror,
You utter cries of shame and terror.
What though to males you look all right?
For heaven's sake, your hair 's a sight.
You hasten to the Gallic lair
Where lurks Maurice, or Jean or Pierre.
Between arrival and departure
You suffer hours of vicious torture,
At last emerging, white and weak,
But sure at least your mane is chic.
Thus you rejoice, my dear, unknowing
That all the time your hair is growing.
The waves so dearly purchasèd
Next month will have grown a foot or so away
    from your head.

III

I 've said, I think, I think we ought
To think at times a sobering thought.

Man's lot it is to be a field
For crops that no nutrition yield,
That filter through his tender skin
And ripen on his head or chin.
I face mankind and shudder, knowing
That everybody's hair is growing;
That lovers, linked in darkened hallways,
Are capped with hair that groweth always;
That millions, shaven in the morning,
At eve find beards their jowls adorning;
That hair is creeping through the scalps
Of yodelers yodeling in the Alps,
And pushing through the epidermises
Of peasants frolicking at kermises;
And poking bravely through the pores
Of cannibals on tropic shores;
That freezing, scorching, raining, snowing,
People's hair is always growing.
I contemplate with dark despair
The awful force of growing hair,
Although admitting, to be quite honest,
That it will be worth a million Niagaras to
        humanity if Science can ever get it harnessed.

One Good Hoarder Deserves Another

' Who is that most attractive man? '
The eager people shout—
More shame on they,
For I 'm sorry to say
It 's Obadiah Stout.
The dowager swaps him compliments,
While the debutante admires;
They rock the globe
With praise of Obe,
The man with four new tires.

Last year he rode downtown alone,
And home alone from dances,
And girls in hordes
With loud O Lords!
Rebuffed his wistful glances.
He humbly crept from snub to snub,
The lowliest of pariahs;
No gaffer or youth
Foresaw, forsooth,
Those tires of Obadiah's.

The two in front are firm to touch,
Their pressure is twenty-eight-pound;
At the turn of a wheel
They never, never squeal;
And the two in back are round.
Oh, others must hobble upon the rim,
Or trudge, as did their sires,
Or swallow their pride
And thumb a ride
From the man with four new tires.

The upper crust of the *crème de la creme*
Hangs on him like a tassel;
The erstwhile bore,
The yokel of yore,
Is now the king of the castle.
For if you do not care to drive
In a jeep, or a Black Maria,
Or take a chance
In an ambulance,
You cultivate Obadiah.

How many hitherto gelid hearts
Glow now with amorous fires!

What traps are planned
For the fair white hand
Of the man with four new tires!
But hark! I hear from the beauty shops
A scream like a wounded cougar—
He has married a girl
With a winsome curl,
And a hundred pounds of sougar.

Coffee with the Meal

A gentlemanly gentleman, as mild as May,
Entered a restaurant famed and gay.
A waiter sat him in a draughty seat
And laughingly inquired what he'd like to eat.
'Oh I don't want venison, I don't want veal,
But I do insist on coffee with the meal.
Bring me clams in a chilly group,
And a large tureen of vegetable soup,
Steak as tender as a maiden's dream,
With lots of potatoes hashed in cream,
And a lettuce and tomato salad, please,
And crackers and a bit of Roquefort cheese,

But waiter, the gist of my appeal,
Is coffee with, coffee with, coffee with the meal.'
The waiter groaned and he wrung his hands;
' Perhaps da headwaiter onderstands.'
Said the sleek headwaiter, like a snobbish seal,
' What, monsieur?   Coffee with the meal? '
His lip drew up in scornful laughter;
' Monsieur desires a demitasse after! '
The gentleman's eyes grew hard as steel,
He said: ' I 'm ordering coffee with the meal.
Hot black coffee in a great big cup,
Fuming, steaming, filled right up.
I don't want coffee iced in a glass,
And I don't want a miserable demitasse,
But what I 'll have, come woe, come weal,
Is coffee with, coffee with, coffee with the meal.'
The headwaiter bowed like a poppy in the breeze;
' Monsieur desires coffee with the salad or the
        cheese? '
Monsieur said: ' Now you 're getting warmer;
Coffee with the latter, coffee with the former;
Coffee with the steak, coffee with the soup,
Coffee with the clams in a chilly group;
Yes, and with a cocktail I could do,

So bring me coffee with the cocktail, too.
I'll fight to the death for my bright ideal,
Which is coffee with, coffee with, coffee with the
    meal.'
The headwaiter swiveled on a graceful heel;
'Certainly, certainly, coffee with the meal!'
The waiter gave an obsequious squeal,
'Yes sir, yes sir, coffee with the meal!'
Oh what a glow did Monsieur feel
At the warming vision of coffee with the meal.
One hour later Monsieur, alas!
Got his coffee in a demitasse.

Just Wrap It Up, and I'll Throw It *Away* Later

Men think that men have more sense than women
    and women think that any woman has more
    sense than any man,
An issue which I eagerly evade, for who am I to
    pass judgment on the comparative reasoning
    processes of, say, Mr. Lunt and Miss Fontanne?
However, I ask you to visualize, please, a clear-
    thinking American male who needs a hat, or a

left sock, or an ashtray in the form of the statue
Civic Virtue by the sculptor MacMonnies,

And what does he do, he goes into the likeliest
shop and buys it and returns to the regular
evening race with the children for first go at
the funnies.

Kindly contrast this with the procedure of his wife
or sister or aunt who drops into a store for
three ounces of flax for the spinning wheel or
an extra minuet for the spinet,

And what happens, the doorstep is crawling for
days with people delivering lampshades and
bedspreads and dirndls and chairs that expand
into bridge tables and bridge tables that
expand into *chaises longues*, and husbands
who can't bear it simply have to grin it.

Man's idea of shopping is to buy what he needs
and get through with it.

Woman's idea is to have everything she has never
needed sent home and then figure out what
to do with it.

It is as true to-day as in the day of David and
Goliath or Corbett and Fitzsimmons,

That men go into a shop to supply a want, and

women principally to stimulate their imaginations, but men's imaginations need no extra stimulus as long as their world is filled with beautiful unanswerable womens.

Anatomical Reflection

Sally Rand
Needs an extra hand.

Dr. Fell? I Thought So

Some people relate anecdotes about Samuel
    Goldwyn and Gregory Ratoff;
I sing of Dr. Fell, who slips in the only vacant
    barber chair while you are taking your hat off.
Does a young man go to a picture with a girl he
    hopes to make a bride of?
The immovable Dr. Fell is what the only two empty
    seats are one on each side of.
You are marooned downtown on a night when the
    rain is a Niagara and the wind is a bayonet,
And after twenty minutes of futile whistling you
    catch a taxi driver's eye and as he slows down

Dr. Fell emerges miraculously from a hydrant,
steps into the cab and drives away in it.
Dr. Fell obviously works with the assistance of a
brownie or a malevolent dwarf,
For it is he who by monopolizing the middle of the
road reaches the ferry ahead of you and slides
into the last space, thus leaving you to two hours'
uninterrupted contemplation of the wharf.
Yes, I fear that Dr. Fell is a monopolist and an
obstructionist,
But I would not grudge him the obstructive
monopoly of that portion of a whirlpool
where the suction is the suctionest.

The Strange Case of Mr. Pauncefoot's Broad Mind

Once there was a man named Mr. Pauncefoot to
whom Fate could not have been meaner,
Because he was a born in-betweener.
Yes, he was one whom in an argument nothing
but woe ever betides,
Because he always thought that there was much to
be said on both sides,

With the result that to his friends on the Left he
    was but a little capitalistic bee busy dis-
    tributing Tory pollen,

While on the Right he was rumored to be in the
    pay of Stalin.

Mr. Pauncefoot lived in a suburb, which was in-
    evitable but rather a pity,

Since the upshot was that he appeared as a city
    boy in the country and a country boy in the
    city.

He was never invited to sing either solo or
    in a convivial quartet by even the kindest
    Samaritan,

Because his voice was just a little too low for the
    tenor and just a little too high for the baritan.

Mr. Pauncefoot was miserable until one day he
    read about the donkey that starved to death
    between two haystacks because it couldn't
    decide which haystack to begin on, and he
    said: 'That's an end of all my confusions,'

Only Mr. Pauncefoot didn't starve to death, quite
    the opposite, he spent the rest of his days
    very happily eating his own words between
    two conclusions.

What Street Is This, Driver?

Let this be my tardy farewell
To the erstwhile Sixth Avenue El.
Though no longer a native New Yorker
My aesthetic eye is a corker;
The El had a twelve-foot clearance
And I notice its disappearance.
New York was to many a kingdom
Where business or pleasure bringdom,
But I got there so seldom
To me 'twas Sixth Avenue Eldom.
It never got any one downer
Than this timid out-of-towner;
It ran like an iron entrail
Midway 'twixt Penn and Grand Central;
It staggered column by column
From the Battery up to Harlem,
And no matter wherever went you
The Sixth Avenue El went too.
You'd be riding from Park to Madison
While leafing through Steele or Addison,
And fleeter than meter could tell
You'd be twisting under the El;

Be you headed south or north
On Lexington, Park or Fourth
Any whither you wished to flit,
Lay the El between you and it.
Farewell, O El, farewell;
I was once of your clientele.
Although I'm no longer Manhattanized
I'm glad that we met and fraternized.
I remember warmly enough
The journeys to Coogan's Bluff,
And the tingling tangling nerve
As we rattled round Suicide Curve;
You could tell by the chuckling sound
That the train was Giant bound.
There was Laughing Larry Doyle
In the days when oil was oil,
And later, when oil was fusel,
We hollered for Emil Meusel.
McGeehan wrote better than Shelley
In descriptions of Long George Kelly;
Hoyt was adroit and hot
And Ott a promising tot,
And I'd rather have met Frankie Frisch
Than marry Lillian Gish;

To win was the only law
And the law was John McGraw.
Ah, then we placed our reliance
On the El and on the Giants;
Now the El with McGraw is buried,
And the torrid Giants are terried,
Now realtors along Sixth Avenue
Anticipate mounting revenue.
No more the El careens
Past intimate family scenes;
Housewives no longer gape
From window and fire escape
At passengers packed like pemmican
Who are gaping back at them again;
Like Wichita, or Los Angeles,
Sixth Ave. is now new-fangelous,
Light as an air by Bizet,
And broad as the Champs Élysées.
Fit for Geddes (Norman Bel)
Is Sixth Avenue minus the El.
This notable civic improvement
Facilitates traffic movement;
It clears the street for sleighs
And the sidewalks for cafés.

O El, thy era is o'er;
I am glad that thou art no more;
But I'd hold myself lower than dirt
Weren't I glad that once thou wert.

Summer Serenade

When the thunder stalks the sky,
When tickle-footed walks the fly,
When shirt is wet and throat is dry,
Look, my darling, that's July.

Though the grassy lawn be leather,
And prickly temper tug the tether,
Shall we postpone our love for weather?
If we must melt, let's melt together!

So Does Everybody Else, Only not So Much

O all ye exorcizers come and exorcise now, and ye
    clergymen draw nigh and clerge,
For I wish to be purged of an urge.
It is an irksome urge, compounded of nettles and
    glue,

And it is turning all my friends back into acquaintances, and all my acquaintances into people who look the other way when I heave into view.

It is an indication that my mental buttery is butterless and my mental larder lardless,

And it consists not of 'Stop me if you've heard this one,' but of 'I know you've heard this one because I told it to you myself, but I'm going to tell it to you again regardless,'

Yes I fear I am living beyond my mental means

When I realize that it is not only anecdotes that I reiterate but what is far worse, summaries of radio programmes and descriptions of cartoons in newspapers and magazines.

I want to resist but I cannot resist recounting the bright sayings of celebrities that everybody already is familiar with every word of;

I want to refrain but cannot refrain from telling the same audience on two successive evenings the same little snatches of domestic gossip about people I used to know that they have never heard of.

When I remember some titillating episode of my childhood I figure that if it's worth narrating

once it's worth narrating twice, in spite of
   lackluster eyes and drooping jaws,
And indeed I have now worked my way backward
   from titillating episodes in my own childhood
   to titillating episodes in the childhood of my
   parents or even my parents-in-laws,
And what really turns my corpuscles to ice,
I carry around clippings and read them to people
   twice.
And I know what I am doing while I am doing it
   and I don't want to do it but I can't help doing
   it and I am just another Ancient Mariner,
And the prospects for my future social life couldn't
   possibly be barrener.
Did I tell you that the prospects for my future social
   life couldn't possibly be barrener?

Homeward Bund

Be careful not to hate the moth,
It isn't she who eats your cloth,
But only little ones of hers
That lunch on tweeds and dine on furs.

Who but a jingo his heart could steel
To spray these innocents out of a meal?
My heart is mush, so come on, larvae,
My closet's full, and I'm Fred Harvey.

Allergy in a Country Churchyard

Once there was a man named Mr. Weaver,
And he had a lot of hay but he didn't have any
    hay fever,
So he ran an advertisement which he wanted to
    charge, but for which he was compelled to pay,
And he advertised that he would like to meet up
    with somebody who had a lot of hay fever
    but didn't have any hay,
So along came a man and he said he had seen his
    ad in the paper,
And was the proposition serious or merely a
    prankish caper,
And Mr. Weaver said it was as serious as the
    dickens,
Because to his mind hay fever was to the human
    race what bumblefoot, limber neck and
    edema of the wattles were to chickens,

And he said he was the most modest of men,

But never having had hay fever he felt very irked
at being outexperienced by any passing
bumblefooted hen,

And the man said I can describe hay fever for you
so you'll know all about it, but first how much
are you prepared to pay?

And Mr. Weaver said: 'Can I charge it?' and the
man said No, so Mr. Weaver said he would
give him all his hay,

So the man said All right and threw pepper in Mr.
Weaver's eyes,

And Mr. Weaver said: 'What are you doing?
and the man said: 'Never mind, just kindly
answer the following questions with the
correct replies,

What's the kind of nut you put back in the dish
at cocktail parties?' and Mr. Weaver said
'A cashew,' and the man said 'Gesundheit.
What material do politicians say their
opponents' lies are composed of?' and Mr.
Weaver said 'The whole cloth,' and the man
said 'No no try again,' and Mr. Weaver said
'A tissue,' and the man said 'Gesundheit.

What 's a filmy collar often worn by women?'
and Mr. Weaver said 'A fichu,' and the man
said 'Gesundheit. Now you know all about
hay fever,'
So he went off with Mr. Weaver's hay, but first he
telephoned an old schoolmate in Vancouver
and charged the call to Mr. Weaver.

Ma, What 's a Banker? or Hush, My Child

The North wind doth blow,
And we shall have snow,
And what will the banker do then, poor thing?
Will he go to the barn
To keep himself warm,
And hide his head under his wing?
Is he on the spot, poor thing, poor thing?
Probably not, poor thing.

For when he is good,
He is not very good,
And when he is bad he is horrider,
And the chances are fair

He is taking the air
Beside a cabaña in Florida.
But the wailing investor, mean thing, mean thing,
Disturbs his siesta, poor thing.

He will plunge in the pool,
But he makes it a rule
To plunge with his kith and his kin,
And whisper about
That it's time to get out
When the widows and orphans get in.
He only got out, poor thing, poor thing,
Yet they call him a tout, poor thing.

His heart simply melts
For every one else;
By love and compassion he's ridden;
The pay of his clerks
To reduce, how it irks!
But he couldn't go South if he didden.
I'm glad there's a drink within reach, poor thing,
As he weeps on the beach, poor thing.

May he some day find peace
In a temple in Greece,

Where the Government harbours no rancour;
May Athens and Sparta
Play host to the martyr,
And purchase a bond from the banker.
With the banker in Greece, poor thing, poor thing,
We can cling to our fleece, Hot Cha!

A Penny Saved Is Impossible

The further through life I drift
The more obvious it becomes that I am lacking in
    thrift.
Now thrift is such a boon to its possessor that
    years ago they began to tax it,
But it is a bane to him that lacks it
Because if you lack it you will go into a shoppe
    and pay two dollars for a gifte,
But if you possess it you find something just as
    good for a dollar fifte.
A penny is merely something that you pull several
    of out of your pocket before you find the
    nickel you need for a telephone call, if
    thriftlessness is in your blood,

Whereas to the thrifty a penny is something to be
    put out at stud.
Thrifty people put two-cent stamps on letters
    addressed to a three-cent zone,
And thriftless people on the other end pay the
    postage due and the thrifty people chuckle
    and rub their hands because the saving on
    every six letters represents a year's interest on
    a dollar loan.
Oh that I were thrifty, because thrifty people leave
    estates to delight their next of kin with;
Oh yes that I were thrifty, because then not only
    would I have money in the bank to pay my
    bills, but I could leave the money in the bank
    because I wouldn't have run up the bills to
    begin with;
Oh that I were not a spendthrift, oh then would
    my heart indeed be gladsome,
Because it is so futile being a spendthrift because I
    don't know any places where thrift could be
    spent even if I had some.

Boo!

The male mosquito fills the air
With threats of eating babies rare;
His humming, like a jackal's bark,
Harrows children in the dark;
But listen, kids, it's all all right,
The male mosquito cannot bite.
Thus we compare the male mosquito
To people who—Why, here's Benito!

Don't Even Tell Your Wife, Particularly

All good men believe that women would rather
    get rid of a piece of gossip than a bulge,
And all good women believe that gossip is a
    feminine weakness in which men never indulge.
Rather than give ear to scandalous rumours,
Why, men would rather play golf in bloomers,
And rather than talk behind each other's backs,
They would go shopping in a mink coat and slacks.
It is one of each sex's uniquenesses
That men's talk is all of humanity's aspirations,
    and women's all of their friends' weaknesses.

Yes, this is a universal credo that no amount of
   evidence can alter,
Including that of Petronius, Suetonius, Pepys,
   Boswell, the locker room of the country club,
   and Mrs. Winchell's little boy, Walter.
Allow me to ask and answer one question before
   departing for Mount Everest or Lake Ossipee:
Who says men aren't gossipy?—Men say men
   aren't gossipy.

What 'll We Do Now? or I'm *Afraid I Know* or *Good Old Just Plain Charades*, Farewell

> I do not know its name,
> Mostly it's called The Game.
>
> Or sometimes Indications,
> Or other variations.
>
> But whatever be its name,
> I was happy ere it came.
>
> But now that it has come,
> I'm a bum.

Figure of fun and shame,
I do not like The Game.

To be honest, to be candid,
I do not understandid;

I amn't very good at it,
I 'm never understood at it.

I am seized by mental gout
When acting phrases out.

I am lost in foggy mazes
When guessing others' phrases.

I 'm a gabbling babbling moron
At quotations from The Koran.

Yea, even Mother Goose's
Leave me stammering excuses.

Be mine, be mine the blame,
But I do not like the game.

Before the game arrived
My social talent thrived.

At chitchat, bridge or poker,
An admitted okeydoker.

A fourteenth at every party
Whether Babbitty or arty.

Where is that talent now?
Inquires this erstwhile wow.

Where is it now? inquiahs
This lowest of pariahs.

And hostesses exclaim
It has vanished with The Game,
The Game without a name,
The Game, The Game, The Game,
You were Beebe ere it came,
But now that it has come
You're a bum.

I do not know its name;
Mostly it's called The Game.

Many enjoy it vastly,
I find it ghastly.

The Phoenix

Deep in the study
Of eugenics
We find that fabled
Fowl, the Phoenix.
The wisest bird
As ever was,
Rejecting other
Mas and Pas,
It lays one egg,
Not ten or twelve,
And when it's hatched,
Out pops itselve.

Here's to You, Little Boy Blue

Sleep is something about which I feel so strongly
    and affectionately that I would fain write a
    song about it,
And I constantly marvel at the great men who have
    been wrong about it.
Critics tell us that there have been few more lucid
    minds than Dr. Johnson's,

Yet it was Dr. Johnson who said: 'Preserve me
from unseasonable and immoderate sleep,'
which is obviously arrant nonsense.

What does he mean 'unseasonable,' does he mean
he only wants to sleep in the winter, like a
groundhog, or through a Beethoven sonata,
like a jitterbug, and does he deem thirteen
hours' sleep a night immoderate?

Why Shakespeare himself, whose mind critics tell
us there have been few more lucid than,
expressly states that 'Sleep knits up the
ravelled sleave of care' and would be the
first to admit that a good thirteen-hour sleep
would not only knit it up but even spell it
correctly and solder it.

Yet even Shakespeare nodded at times, for did he
not write 'To sleep: perchance to dream: ay,
there's the rub'? Well, he must have
written those lines either to Sweeney or the
marines or the Thibetan navy,

Because to dream is not the rub, it's the gravy,

Because I know a man, he can't throw a baseball
any harder than your granddaughter can blow
a bubble,

And he dreamed he was pitching for the Giants
against Brooklyn and he shut them out with
one hit and it would have been a no-hitter
only Mel Ott misjudged an easy fly with two
out in the ninth and it rolled through his
legs for a double,
But he fanned Medwick on two pitched balls to
end the game, so this dream not only pleased
him but also helped the Giants' box office
quite a lot,
Because now whenever this man is awake he goes
up to the Polo Grounds not because he expects
to get to pitch again, but just to boo Ott.
So about the greatness of Shakespeare and Dr.
Johnson I do not wish to hear another peep,
Because for my money no man is greater than his
respect for sleep.

The Jellyfish

Who wants my jellyfish?
I 'm not sellyfish!

Once there was a couple named Mr. and Mrs.
    Pepperloaf and they were simply devoted,
Because each other was upon what they doted,
And in Mrs. Pepperloaf's eyes Mr. Pepperloaf
    could never err,
And he admitted only one flaw in her,
But it was a flaw which took many virtues to assuage,
Consisting in always asking him the date while
    she was reading the paper with the date
    clearly printed on every page,
And whenever he called her attention to this least
    admirable of her traits
She would retort that he didn't trust the paper's
    weather forecasts so then why should she
    trust its dates?
For eleven years his patience held
But finally he rebelled.
It was on the evening of Friday the seventh that
    she looked up from her paper and asked him
    the date,
And he replied firmly that she would find it at the
    top of the page so she looked at the top of

the page and that was that, and presently they sat down to supper and ate,

And they were miserable because they had never disagreed and this contretemps was a beginner for them,

And at nine his employer's wife called up to ask where were they, she and eleven guests were waiting dinner for them,

And Mr. Pepperloaf asked Mrs. Pepperloaf how she could have so misreckoned,

And she said she knew that they had been invited out on the seventh but, according to the newspaper he had instructed her to consult, to-night was only the second,

And he picked up the paper and it was last week's, not to-day's,

And she said certainly, she had just been reading over some recipes for different delicious soufflés,

And now she found the first flaw in him because she had obeyed his order to look for the date in the paper, hadn't she, so his irritation was uncalled for and unseasonable.

Women would rather be right than reasonable.

The Caraway Seed

The Abbé Voltaire, alias Arouet,
Never denounced the seed of the caraway;
Sufficient proof, if proof we need,
That he never bit into a caraway seed.

Don't Shoot Los Angeles

Is it true what they say about Los Angeles, that
    Los Angeles is erratic,
That in the sweet national symphony of common
    sense Los Angeles is the static?
Yes it is true, Los Angeles is not only erratic, not
    only erotic,
Los Angeles is crotchety, centrifugal, vertiginous,
    esoteric and exotic.
Many people blame the movies and the movie
    makers for Los Angeles's emotional rumpus,
But they are mistaken, it is the compass.
Certainly Los Angeles is a cloudburst of non-
    sequiturs, and of logic a drouth,
But what can you expect of a city that is laid out
    east and west instead of north and south?

Mother Nature knows best,
And it was Mother Nature who decreed that all
   sensible things run north and south, not east
   and west.
North is uphill and south is downhill, which is
   why where a river springs forth,
That 's north,
And where 's its mouth,
That 's south,
Which is why the Los Angeles mind does not
   function in the normal true and tried ways,
Because their city runs east and west instead of
   north and south so they approach every
   decision sideways.
The only solution is for Los Angeles to pivot,
And I imagine the Chamber of Commerce will
   replace the divot.

Celery

Celery, raw,
Develops the jaw,
But celery, stewed,
Is more quietly chewed.

Some people are born simply to pay postage due,
Which is like being born simply to tread on the
    gum that other people chew.
Anybody sensible
Knows that the demand for extra postage heralds the
    arrival of tidings unconditionally dispensable;
There is no instance thus far
Of a postage-due envelope having contained either
    a check or a confession of murder or an in-
    vitation to dine with Winston Churchill and
    Hedy Lamarr;
Yet who so thrifty
As not to pay their own weight in pennies annually
    to discover that a new grocery store will open
    week before last, or that they owe an old
    grocery store eleven-fifty?
It is postage-due mail that requests your presence
    at a benefit and encloses two tickets that will
    be charged to you unless you write a letter
    returning them to the requester;
It is postage-due mail that electrifies you with a
    full report of the graduation exercises at the

kindergarten that you attended, while going
    on five, for one semester.
Yet such is the fascination of getting nothing for
    something that whenever the postman whistles,
People pour forth to proffer good money for mis-
    directed and understamped epistles.
I know a man whose moral sense is checkered,
And next to looking through keyholes he likes
    reading other people's mail, but not their
    postage-due mail, he says he'd rather browse
    in the *Congressional Record*.

Assorted Chocolates

If some confectioner were willing
To let the shape announce the filling,
We'd encounter fewer assorted chocs,
Bitten into and returned to the box.

Out Is Out

Come in, dear guests, we've got a treat for you,
We've prepared a different place to eat for you!
Guess where we're going to have our dinner!
Every one guess! Who'll be the winner?

The dining room? Heavens! It's hereby stated
That dining rooms are dreadfully dated.
What in the world could be more plebeian
Than to eat in a place in which you can see in!
The living room? No, you're off the path;
No, not the bedroom; no, not the bath;
And not the cellar; and not the attic;
The kitchen? No, that's too democratic.
Do you all give up? Well, listen and hark:
We're going to dine outdoors, in the dark!
We're going to dine outdoors, on the terrace,
As dark as an Anti-kink heir or heiress.
No lights, because there aren't any plugs,
And anyhow, lights attract the bugs,
And anyhow, in the dark we've found
There are bugs enough to go around.
Oh, it's drizzling a little; I think perhaps
The girls had better keep on their wraps;
Just strike a match and enjoy the way
The raindrops splash in the consommé.
You probably won't get botts or pellagra
From whatever lit on your pâté de foie gras.
Now, you're not expected to eat with skill,
And everybody's supposed to spill;

*G   189

If your half-broiled chicken leaps about,
That's half the excitement of eating out;
If you dust it with sugar instead of salt,
It's every one's fun and nobody's fault;
And if anything flies in your mouth, perchance,
Why, that is mystery, that's romance!
Such a frolic and such a lark
It is to eat outdoors in the dark!
The dandiest fun since I don't know when;
Would you eat in a stuffy old room again?
Oh yes you would, you lukewarm liars,
And I'll see you to-morrow at the cleaner's and dyer's.

Practically a Summary of Practically Autumn

September is a curious month,
It has no sense at all, yet.
It's not precisely summer,
But it's not exactly fall, yet.

A curious month September is.
Its weather is its highlight;
You roll your shirt sleeves up at noon
And don your furs at twilight.

September is a curious month.
It made the nations brothers
By awarding one the Davis Cup
And enraging all the others.

A curious month September is.
Its sports will not stay put, now;
Among its ball games, half are base—
And half of them are foot—now.

September is a curious month.
With winter drawing sooner,
The ladies buy new thingamajigs
Not Decemberer, but Juner.

A curious month September is.
Regret is what it ends with,
And yet relief is partly what
We part from summer friends with.

September is a curious month,
Which I wouldn't part with a day from.
It makes you glad to get back to where
You were glad to get away from.

Get Up, Fellows, It's Time to Go to Bed

It's more than logical, it's biological,

To be lethargical,

And contrariwise it's abecedarian, or childishly
alphabetic,

That it's ridiculous to be energetic.

Welcome, lassitude!

Scram, vivacitude!

Up with the grasshopper and the sluggard!

Away with the ant and the bee and all individualists
whether puny or ruggard!

Before our ancestors were apes they were
fish,

But they improved their condition and got to be
human beings and founded a lot of empires
such as the ancient Persian and Roman and
the contemporary Brish,

But the ocean to-day with us would be brimming

If our ancestors hadn't had sense enough to stop
all that continuous swimming,

Whereas now we can ride up and down in elevators
and go to the movies, and fish are only something about which some people say: 'Yum

yum, right out of the water and fried to a
delicate golden brown,'
And the only reason the fish aren't eating the people
instead of the people eating the fish is that
fish can't do two things that have got people
where they are, they can't close their eyes and
they can't sit down.

The Parsnip

The parsnip, children, I repeat,
Is simply an anemic beet.
Some people call the parsnip edible;
Myself, I find this claim incredible.

I Burn Money

The song about the happy-go-lucky fellow who
hasn't time to be a millionaire strikes me as
pretty funny,
Because I am pretty happy-go-lucky myself but it
isn't lack of time that keeps me from being a
millionaire, it's lack of money,
But if anybody has a million that they're through
with it,

Well, I know what I'd like to do with it.

My first acquisition would not be a lot of Old Masters or first editions or palatial palaces,

No, it would be to supply each of my pairs of pants with its own set of galluses.

I can also think of another extravagance with which to startle all beholders

Which is an attendant with no other duties than to apply antisunburn lotion to that vulnerable spot you can't get at yourself either by reaching over or under your shoulders.

Likewise I have an idea which should earn the gratitude of every regular-dinner eater alive,

Which is to promote a regular-dinner that when you order oysters or clams on it you get six oysters or clams instead of five.

My next goal is one to reach which I should probably have to sink into debt,

But it would be worth it because it is the development of a short, hot, harsh, quick-burning, full-of-nicotine cigarette.

A million dollars could also be well spent in hiring somebody to invent some better rhymes for wife than rife and knife and strife,

But I think what I would really do if I had a million
would be to buy a million dollars' worth of
books written by me and then besides having
a lot of good books I could sit back and live
on the royalties for the rest of my life.

Who's Going Mr. Platt's Way?

So it comes to pass
That you double up with the neighbours to save
rubber and gas,
And who are you to pity that celluloid dog in
pursuit of that asbestos cat?
Your automobile-mate turns out to be nice old
Mr. Platt,
And nice old Mr. Platt is no Casey Jones, he is even
no nice old Judge Hardy,
When he calls for you he is fifteen minutes early,
and when you call for him he is fifteen
minutes tardy,
And he has worn a depression in the front seat of
your car, but in his, no matter how you
fumble,

Well, somehow you always end up with your
    knees against your chin back in his roofed-in
    rumble,
And if you are driving, why the task of pointing
    out oncoming vehicles and curves is one he
    is too conscientious to spurn,
And if he is driving he never remembers where he
    wants to turn left until he is halfway past the
    left turn,
And it's an odd thing about nice old Mr. Platt
    and the crack of dawn,
Because if you find an evening tedious, the crack
    of dawn is the moment to which he intends
    to linger on,
While if you are enjoying yourself, at nine o'clock
    he will smother a yawn,
And explain that he is sorry to drag you away but
    unfortunately he has an important engage-
    ment at the crack of dawn.
Oh well, I guess that's that—
Some people are doubled up with ptomaine, and
    other people are doubled up with nice old
    Mr. Platt.

A Drink with Something in It

There is something about a Martini,
A tingle remarkably pleasant;
A yellow, a mellow Martini;
I wish that I had one at present.
There is something about a Martini,
Ere the dining and dancing begin,
And to tell you the truth,
It is not the vermouth—
I think that perhaps it 's the Gin.

There is something about an old-fashioned
That kindles a cardiac glow;
It is soothing and soft and impassioned
As a lyric by Swinburne or Poe.
There is something about an old-fashioned
When dusk has enveloped the sky,
And it may be the ice,
Or the pineapple slice,
But I strongly suspect it 's the Rye.

There is something about a mint julep.
It is nectar imbibed in a dream,

As fresh as the bud of the tulip,
As cool as the bed of the stream.
There is something about a mint julep,
A fragrance beloved by the lucky.
And perhaps it 's the tint
Of the frost and the mint,
But I think it was born in Kentucky.

There is something they put in a highball
That awakens the torpidest brain,
That kindles a spark in the eyeball,
Gliding singing through vein after vein.
There is something they put in a highball
Which you 'll notice one day, if you watch;
And it may be the soda,
But judged by the odor,
I rather believe it 's the Scotch.

Then here 's to the heartening wassail,
Wherever good fellows are found;
Be its master instead of its vassal,
And order the glasses around.
Oh, it 's Beer if you 're bent on expansion,
And Wine if you wish to grow thin,

But quaffers who think
Of a drink as a drink,
When they quaff, quaff of Whisky and Gin.

The Porpoise

I kind of like the playful porpoise,
A healthy mind in a healthy corpus.
He and his cousin, the playful dolphin,
Why they like swimmin like I like golphin.

The Shark

How many Scientists have written
The shark is gentle as a kitten!
Yet this I know about the shark:
His bite is worser than his bark.

Water for the Gander

You take a man who has ever possessed an infant
    son or daughter,
And he feels pretty superior about drinks of water.
His voice is full of paternal lenience
As he describes how their thirst is always adjusted
    to his utmost inconvenience,

And you gather that there is no rest for the married,

If only because of the little ones who choose to be perpetually inopportunely arid.

I assume that these little ones have never seen their sire in session

At his business or profession,

So listen closely, infant son and infant daughter,

His business or profession is what he carries on between getting up to get a drink of water.

It requires a dozen visits to the nearest water cooler or fount

Before he can face drawing up a report or balancing an account.

You may be interested to note

That the driest point in America is not Death Valley, but a man with lots of important work on his desk's throat.

Therefore, children, when he next complains at midnight about your everlasting thirst,

Simply ask him how many hours he spent that day at his desk and how many at the water cooler, and he may answer you, but I bet he has to go and get himself a drink of water first.

The Cantaloupe

One cantaloupe is ripe and lush,
Another's green, another's mush.
I'd buy a lot more cantaloupe
If I possessed a fluoroscope.

I Don't Mean Us, Except Occasionally

I know a man who when he bares his breast to life
    it comes back to him all covered with welts,
Because everything that happens to him is much
    worse than the same thing happening to any-
    body else.
Other people with a cold just have colds, but
    when he has a cold it combines pneumonia
    and dropsy and tropical fever,
And he greets any attempt to cheer him up with the
    frigid politeness of a retiring Chairman of the
    Board saying How do you do to the newly
    appointed Receiver.
Other people with indigestion just have indi-
    gestion, but his indigestion ranks somewhere
    between appendicitis and cholera,

And his medicine chest is clogged with various
gastric appeasers costing from fifty cents a
bottle up to a dollar a.
He is the man for whom the razor-blade people
manufacture that special individual teaspoon-
edged blade for,
And the man who never discovers that his new
shoes don't fit until immediately after they
are paid for.
Everybody is always running around with bushels
with which to hide his talents,
And he is the only depositor in the world for
whom his bank employs a special staff of
certified private accountants just to keep his
bank book out of balance.
I really don't see how that man remains perpendi-
cular,
And I am glad that I am not at all like him, except
in many a particular.

The Octopus

Tell me, O Octopus, I begs,
Is those things arms, or is they legs?
I marvel at thee, Octopus;
If I were thou, I 'd call me Us.

Has Anybody Seen My Noumenon? [1]

There is one point which I am more than human
    on,
And that 's a noumenon.
On due reflection we are apt to find
That it is noumenons which lead us to believe that
    just this once two pair will beat three of a kind.
It is noumenons which whisper to our hearts that
    our futures will be brighter than our yores,
And noumenons which encourage us to laugh off
    the black clouds in the west and go ahead
    and move the supper table out of doors.
It is noumenons which convince you that you can

---

[1] Noumenon, n., an object known only by
intuition, apart from any evidence of the senses.

meet the next tax installment without having set aside the sum that is requisite,

And noumenons which stir the fancy that M. Laval may some day reject an order from Berlin with a cry of ' Ze hequisite.'

It is noumenons which, if you have no excuse for flouting natural laws, they supply it,

Such as kindling the hope that you can remain trim and lissome at forty without the nuisance of exercise or diet,

So now I shall go out and consume a hearty lunch,

But I know I shall remain trim and lissome in spite of it, because I have a strong noumenon, or overwhelming hunch.

The Mermaid

Say not the mermaid is a myth,
I knew one once named Mrs. Smith.
She stood while playing cards or knitting;
Mermaids are not equipped for sitting.

A Bulletin Has Just Come In

The rabbit's dreamy eyes grow dreamier
As he quietly gives you tularemia.

The parrot clashes his hooked proboscis
And laughs while handing you psittacosis.

In every swamp or wooded area
Mosquito witches brew malaria.

We risk at every jolly picnic
Spotted fever from a tick nick.

People perish of bubonic;
To rats, it's better than a tonic.

The hog converted into pork
Puts trichinosis on your fork.

The dog to-day that guards your babies
To-morrow turns and gives them rabies.

The baby, once all milk and spittle,
Grows to a Hitler, and boy, can he hittle!

That's our planet, and we're stuck with it.
I wish its inheritors the best of luck with it.

The world contains so many beautiful things to
gaze at
That gazing is an occupation that you could spend
days at,
And these beautiful things are of so many different
kinds, or shall we say heterogeneous,
Such as the sun and moon etc. and butterflies and
mermaids etc., that to list them all you would
have to be an etcetera genius,
So I shall hasten to a landing
And mention two beautiful things that are to my
mind outstanding,
And one of them is to be on a train,
And see what we see when we flatten our noses
against the pane,
And the other is wistful enough to make anybody
feel cosmic and pious,
Which is to stand beside the track and wave at the
passengers as they rocket by us,
So that is why rather than be an etcetera or any
other kind of genius
I would rather be schizophrenious,

Because I should regard it as the most satisfactory
    of stunts
To be able to split my personality and be in two
    places at once,
For who could be so happy as I
Sitting with my nose against a train window
    watching me wave to me as I go rocketing by?

The Eel

I don't mind eels
Except as meals.

Brakeman, Hand Me My Niblick

Once there was a golfer named Mr. Brownie and
    he was a duffer,
And he used to suffer,
But I don't want to be misunderstood,
He suffered chiefly not because he was bad but
    because he thought he was good,
Because his regular game was 101 and if he had
    never broken 100 his disposition would have
    been fine,

But one day eleven years ago playing winter rules
    with a following wind and a dozen conceded
    putts he turned in an 89.
Since when he has never been the same,
Because he has ever since been off his game.
And once there was a railroad named the Baltimore
    and Tomsk and it too had grandiose delusions,
And it jumped at conclusions,
And although no one to the B. & T. than I could
    be loyaler,
I am sorry that they once made a four-hour non-
    stop run between Tomsk and Baltimore with a
    locomotive and baggage car, paced by a motor
    cycle, with the engineer smoking marihuana,
    and benzedrine in the boiler,
Because now they think they can dispatch a
    fourteen-car train with six scheduled stops
    and a flag stop and its time between Tomsk
    and Baltimore will still be the same,
And they quote four hours as their regular running
    time just as Mr. Brownie quotes 89 as his
    regular game.
Does it please you, dear B. & T., that your time-table
    should be Mr. Brownie's score-card's mate?

Remember that a passenger would rather arrive
   on time on a four-hour-and-fifty-minute
   schedule than expect a four-hour trip and
   arrive fifty minutes late.

The Wasp

The wasp and all his numerous family
I look upon as a major calamity.
He throws open his nest with prodigality,
But I distrust his waspitality.

Let Me Buy This One

Solomon said, Stay me with apples for I am sick
   with l'amour,
But I say, Comfort me with flagons, for I am sick
   with rich people talking and acting poor.
I have never yet met even a minor Croesus
Whose pocket-book didn't have paresis;
I have never yet been out with a tycoon for an
   evening in Manhattan's glamorous canyons
When the evening's bills weren't paid by the
   tycoon's impoverished but proud companions.

There is one fact of life that no unwealthy child
    can learn too soon,
Which is that no tycoon ever spends money except
    on another tycoon.
Rich people are people that you owe something to
    and take out to dinner and the theater and
    dancing and all the other expensive things
    there are because you know they are accus-
    tomed to the best and as a result you spend
    the following month on your uppers,
And it is a big evening to you but just another
    evening to them and they return the hos-
    pitality by saying that someday you must drop
    in to one of their cold Sunday suppers.
Rich people are also people who spend most of
    their time complaining about the income tax
    as one of life's greatest and most intolerable
    crosses,
And eventually you find that they haven't even
    paid any income tax since 1929 because their
    income has shrunk to fifty thousand dollars
    a year and everything has been charged off to
    losses,
And your own income isn't income at all, it is

salary, and stops coming in as soon as you stop labouring mentally and manually,

But you have been writing out checks for the Government annually,

So the tax situation is just the same as the entertainment situation because the poor take their little pittance

And pay for the rich's admittance

Because it is a great truth that as soon as people have enough coupons in the safe-deposit vault or in the cookie-jar on the shelf,

Why they don't have to pay anything themself,

No, they can and do just take all their coins and store them,

And other people beg to pay for everything for them,

And they certainly are allowed to,

Because to accept favors is the main thing that the poor are and the rich aren't too proud to,

So let us counterattack with sangfroid and phlegm,

And I propose a Twenty-second Amendment to the Constitution providing that the rich must spend as much money on us poor as we do on them.

Not George Washington's, not Abraham Lincoln's, but Mine

Well, here I am thirty-eight,
Well, I certainly thought I 'd have longer to wait,
You just stop in for a couple of beers,
And gosh, there go thirty-seven years.
Well, it has certainly been fun,
But I certainly thought I 'd have got a lot more
    done.
Why if I had been really waked up and alive,
I could have been a Congressman since I was
    twenty-one or President since I was thirty-five.
I guess I know the reason my accomplishments are
    so measly:
I don't comprehend very easily.
It finally dawned on me that in life's race I was
    off to a delayed start
When at the age of thirty-three I had to be told
    that I could swim faster if I 'd keep my fingers
    together instead of spreading them apart,
And I was convinced that precociousness was not
    the chief of my faults
When it was only last winter that I discovered

that the name of that waltz that skaters waltz
to is 'The Skaters' Waltz.'
After thirty-seven years I find myself the kind of
man that anybody can sell anything to,
And nobody will ever tell anything to.
Whenever people get up a party of which I am to
be a member to see some picture which I
don't want to see because I am uninterested
in the situation that Scarlett and Mr. Chips are
estranged over,
Why my head is what it is arranged over.
Contrariwise, I myself not only can't sell anybody
anything,
I can't even tell anybody anything.
I have never yet had a good gossip bomb all poised
and ready to burst
That somebody hasn't already told everybody first.
Yes, my career to date has certainly been a fiasco;
It would not have made a thrilling dramatic pro-
duction for the late Oliver Morosco or the
late David Belasco.
But in spite of the fact that my career has been a
fiasco to date,
Why I am very proud and happy to be thirty-eight.

The Kangaroo

O Kangaroo, O Kangaroo,
Be grateful that you 're in the zoo,
And not transmuted by a boomerang
To zestful tangy Kangaroo meringue.

Don't Wait, Hit Me Now!

If there are any wives present who wish to irritate
    their husbands or husbands who wish to
    irritate their wives,
Why I know an irritation more irritating than hives,
So if you think such an irritation expedient,
Here is the formula, in which the presence of a
    third person is the only essential extra in-
    gredient;
Indeed it is beautifully simple,
But it is guaranteed to make a molehill out of a
    dimple
And what it consists of is that when you are
    annoyed with your husband or wife and want
    to do the opposite of woo them,

Why, you just talk at them instead of to them.

Suppose you think your Gregory danced too often
     with Mrs. Limbworthy at the club, you don't
     say to him directly: 'Gregory, I'll smack you
     down if you don't lay off that platinum-
     plated hussy,'

No, you wait till a friend drops in and then with
     a glance at Gregory say to her: 'Isn't it funny
     what fools middle-aged men can make of
     themselves over anything blonde and slithery,
     do you understand how anybody sober and
     in their right mind could look twice at that
     Limbworthy job, but then of course darling,
     Gregory wasn't altogether in his right mind
     last night, was he?'

This is indeed more excruciating to Gregory than
     Shakespearian excursions and alarums,

Because there is no defense against caroms.

Or let us suppose you are irked by your Esmeralda's
     sudden passion for antiques,

Well you don't mention it for weeks,

No, you wait till a friend drops in and then with
     a glance at Esmeralda you say: 'How anybody
     can be sucked in by this antique racket is

beyond me, but there are some otherwise sensible women who 'll mortgage their beauty treatments for a genuine early American paper doily or a guaranteed second-hand Killarney banshee,

But of course Esmeralda can't ever resist an opportunity to pick up some fossil to amaze her friends with, can she? '

And Esmeralda must sit quiet and take it with apparent docility,

Because the hit direct doesn't compare with the ricochet in deadly unanswerability.

By this easy method can every Gregory score off every Esmeralda and every Esmeralda annihilate every Gregory,

And its only drawback besides eventual divorce is that it reduces all their friends to emotional beggary.

Further Reflection on Parsley

Parsley
Is gharsley.

Waiting for the Birdie

Some hate broccoli, some hate bacon,
I hate having my picture taken.
How can your family claim to love you
And then demand a picture of you?
The electric chair is a queasy chair,
But I know an equally comfortless pair;
One is the dentist's, my good sirs,
And the other is the photographer's.
Oh, the fly in all domestic ointments
Is affectionate people who make appointments
To have your teeth filled left and right,
Or your face reproduced in black and white.
You open the door and you enter the studio,
And you feel less cheerio than nudio.
The hard light shines like seventy suns,
And you know that your features are foolish ones.
The photographer says, Natural, please,
And you cross your knees and uncross your knees.
Like a duke in a high society chronicle
The camera glares at you through its monocle
And you feel ashamed of your best attire,
Your nose itches, your palms perspire,

Your muscles stiffen, and all the while
You smile and smile and smile and smile.
It 's over; you weakly grope for the door;
It 's not; the photographer wants one more.
And if this experience you survive,
Wait, just wait till the proofs arrive.
You look like a drawing by Thurber or Bab,
Or a gangster stretched on a marble slab.
And all your dear ones, including your wife,
Say There he is, that 's him to the life!
Some hate broccoli, some hate bacon,
But I hate having my picture taken.

I 'll Write Their Number Down When We Get Home

Words, idle words, are what people's social life
    contains a goodly store of,
And the idlest words are contained in the wishful
    phrase beginning, Why don't we see more of?
By the time your age is medium,
Well, your most exotic evenings are placid to the
    point of tedium,
Because whenever you step out you find yourself

stepping out amid faces and ideas that are, to say the least, familiar,

Which is a situation which moves only from the willy-nilly to the willy-nillier,

But once in every eleven blue moons you encounter a newcomer in your little coterie,

And it doesn't matter whether he is a veteran or a veterinary or a vestryman or a vegetarian or a notable or a Notogaean or a notary,

Because his fresh point of view is as beneficial to anemic conversation as a transfusion or a tonic,

And his wife is equally attractive and stimulating, and the future would be cute as a button if it weren't so inevitably ironic,

Because on the way home you say: 'My I like those people, why don't we see more of them?' and it is agreed that Yes we certainly must, and from then on they might as well be living in the ancient Anglian kingdom of Mercia,

Because you never see them again because you never do anything about it except to murmur: 'Why don't we see more of them?' and that is why the best definition I can think of for at least one man's social life is simply inertia.

The Fly

God in His wisdom made the fly
And then forgot to tell us why.

Ask Daddy, He Won't Know

Now that they 've abolished chrome work
I'd like to call their attention to home work.
Here it is only three decades since my scholarship
     was famous,
And I'm an ignoramus.
I cannot think which goes sideways and which
     goes up and down, a parallel or a meridian,
Nor do I know the name of him who first trans-
     lated the Bible into Indian, I see him only as
     an enterprising colonial Gideon.
I have difficulty with dates,
To say nothing of the annual rainfall of the Southern
     Central States,
And the only way I can distinguish proper from
     improper fractions
Is by their actions.

Naturally the correct answers are just back of the
    tip of my tongue,
But try to explain that to your young.
I am overwhelmed by their erudite banter,
I am in no condition to differentiate between
    Timoshenko and Tam o' Shanter.
I reel, I sway, I am utterly exhausted;
Should you ask me when Chicago was founded I
    could only reply I didn't even know it was losted.

The Boy Who Laughed at Santa Claus

In Baltimore there lived a boy.
He wasn't anybody's joy.
Although his name was Jabez Dawes,
His character was full of flaws.
In school he never led his classes,
He hid old ladies' reading glasses,
His mouth was open when he chewed,
And elbows to the table glued.

He stole the milk of hungry kittens,
And walked through doors marked NO ADMIT-
    TANCE.

He said he acted thus because
There wasn't any Santa Claus.
Another trick that tickled Jabez
Was crying 'Boo!' at little babies.
He brushed his teeth, they said in town,
Sideways instead of up and down.

Yet people pardoned every sin,
And viewed his antics with a grin,
Till they were told by Jabez Dawes:
'There isn't any Santa Claus!'
Deploring how he did behave,
His parents swiftly sought their grave.
They hurried through the portals pearly,
And Jabez left the funeral early.

Like whooping cough, from child to child,
He sped to spread the rumor wild:
'Sure as my name is Jabez Dawes
There isn't any Santa Claus!'
Slunk like a weasel or a marten
Through nursery and kindergarten,
Whispering low to every tot:
'There isn't any, no there's not!'

The children wept all Christmas Eve
And Jabez chortled up his sleeve.
No infant dared hang up his stocking
For fear of Jabez' ribald mocking.
He sprawled on his untidy bed,
Fresh malice dancing in his head,
When presently with scalp a-tingling,
Jabez heard a distant jingling;
He heard the crunch of sleigh and hoof
Crisply alighting on the roof.

What good to rise and bar the door?
A shower of soot was on the floor.
What was beheld by Jabez Dawes?
The fireplace full of Santa Claus!
Then Jabez fell upon his knees
With cries of 'Don't,' and 'Pretty please.'
He howled: 'I don't know where you read it,
But anyhow, I never said it!'

'Jabez,' replied the angry saint,
'It isn't I, it's you that ain't.
Although there is a Santa Claus,
There isn't any Jabez Dawes!'

Said Jabez then with impudent vim:
' Oh, yes there is; and I am him!
Your magic don't scare me, it doesn't '—
And suddenly he found he wasn't!

From grimy feet to unkempt locks
Jabez became a jack-in-the-box,
An ugly, vastly ghastly jack
In Santa Claus's bulging pack.
The neighbors heard his mournful squeal;
They searched for him, but not with zeal.
No trace was found of Jabez Dawes,
Which led to thunderous applause,
And people drank a loving cup
And went and hung their stockings up.

All you who sneer at Santa Claus,
Beware the fate of Jabez Dawes,
The saucy boy who mocked the saint.
Donder and Blitzen licked off his paint.

The Termite

Some primal termite knocked on wood
And tasted it, and found it good,
And that is why your Cousin May
Fell through the parlor floor to-day.

Fahrenheit Gesundheit

Nothing is glummer
Than a cold in the summer.
A summer cold
Is to have and to hold.
A cough in the fall
Is nothing at all,
A winter snuffle
Is lost in the shuffle,
And April sneezes
Put leaves on the treeses,
But a summer cold
Is to have and to hold.
Though golf course and beach
Slip beyond your reach,

By a fate grotesque
You can get to your desk,
And there is no rescue
From this germ grotesque.
You can feel it coming,
In your nasal plumbing,
But there is no plumber
For a cold in the summer.
Nostrilly, tonsilly,
It prowls irresponsilly;
In your personal firmament
Its abode is permanent.
Oh, would it were curable
Rather than durable;
Were it Goering's or Himmler's,
Or somebody simlar's!
O Laval, were it thine!
But it isn't, it 's mine.
A summer cold
Is to have and to hold.

Heil, Heilige Nacht!

How many years to Bethlehem?
Near a hundred score.
Can I get there by candlelight?
Not this war.

The friendly, holy candle light
Is bale fire now to death,
Its perilous glimmer long blown out
By sirens' breath.

Through skies the Wise Men humbly scanned
Three keener hunters flit—
Heinkel and Dornier seek the gleam,
With Messerschmitt.

No manger now, no cattle shed,
Too lowly to be found.
Take up the babe and hurry him
Deep underground.

But cave nor grave is deep enough
To shield young flesh and bone.
Hurry him down, and o'er his head
Roll the great stone.

What need of law to still the bells,
For how should bells be merry?
The day the child in joy was born,
The child we bury.

Gentlemen of the High Command,
Who crucify the slums,
There was an earlier Golgotha.
The third day comes.